D0929865

EX LIBRIS
PACE COLLEGE
WESTCHESTER

PLEASANTVILLE, NEW YORK

The
Garland Library
of
War and Peace

The
Garland Library
of
War and Peace

Under the General Editorship of
Blanche Wiesen Cook, *John Jay College, C.U.N.Y.*
Sandi E. Cooper, *Richmond College, C.U.N.Y.*
Charles Chatfield, *Wittenberg University*

The
Church and War

A Catholic Study

by

Franziskus Stratmann

with a new introduction
for the Garland Edition by
Gerard A. Vanderhaar

Garland Publishing, Inc., New York & London
1971

The new introduction for this
Garland Library Edition is Copyright © 1971, by
Garland Publishing Inc.
24 West 45 St., New York, N.Y. 10036

———————

All Rights Reserved

———————

International Standard Book No. ISBN 0-8240-0434-5

Library of Congress No. LC 72-147677

Printed in the United States of America

6.2.
07
71

Introduction

The Christian Church's compromising attitude toward war has been seriously strained in the twentieth century. The ancient Just War Theory, born when the Church became acceptable to the Roman Empire and nourished by the agile minds of scholastic theologians in their cloisters, has been hopelessly inadequate to cope with this century's widely destructive wars. Many thoughtful, concerned people have come to see the Just War Theory for what it originally was, a compromise between the spirit of the Gospels and the demands of politics.

I

The Church began in the echo of the Sermon on the Mount: "You have heard that it was said, 'You shall love your neighbor and hate your enemy.' But I say to you, Love your enemies and pray for those who persecute you" (Matt. 5:43-44). "You have heard that it was said, 'An eye for an eye and a tooth for a tooth.' But I say to you, Do not resist one who is evil. But if any one strikes you on the right cheek, turn to him the other also" (Matt. 5:38-39). The Church remembered that when Jesus was about to be

5

forcibly taken away to an illegal death sentence he refused Peter's defense. "Put your sword back into its place; for all who take the sword shall perish by the sword" (Matt. 26:51-52).

The early Christians generally were unwilling to take part in the military activities of the Roman Empire. They were convinced that the Christian law of love called them to peace, and that killing was incompatible with this law. Justin Martyr wrote, around the year 150, "We who were filled with war and mutual slaughter and every wickedness have each of us in all the world changed our weapons of war . . . swords into plows and spears into agricultural implements" (Trypho, CX). Tertullian, several decades later, was equally explicit. "Christ in disarming Peter ungirt every soldier" (De Idolatria, XIX).

This Christian attitude was known in Rome and regarded as harmful to the Empire. In the middle of the third century Origen quoted Celsus, a critic of Christianity, as saying, "If all men were to do the same as you, there would be nothing to prevent the king from being left in utter solitude and desertion, and the forces of the empire would fall into the hands of the wildest and most lawless barbarians." Origen responded, "We do our ruler better service than do those who bear the sword. . . . Truly, we do not go with him into the battlefield, not even if he commands it, but we fight for him in our camp, a camp of holiness wherein we pray to God" (Contra

Celsum, *VIII*).

When Constantine in the fourth century made the Church respectable, Christianity began to turn from a fringe sect into the official religion of the Roman Empire. Christians came to see themselves as part of the political and social establishment. They were concerned lest, if the Empire fell, the Church should fall also, or at least lose the tremendous gains it had made. The progress of the Church was thought to be linked with political stability; hence Rome had to be defended when it was threatened by barbarian invasions.

Saint Augustine in the early years of the fifth century formulated conditions under which a war was justified and Christians could legitimately fight in it. "War should be waged only as a necessity," he wrote, "and waged only that through it God may deliver men from that necessity and preserve them in peace" (Epist. 189,6). "Love (of enemies) does not exclude wars of mercy waged by the good" (Epist. 138, ii, 15). One could love his enemy and still kill him. In fact, said Saint Augustine, a Christian soldier ought not to kill his enemy unless he did love him! The compromise had begun.

During the Middle Ages the Church was so involved with the political situation that it had to accept war as a legitimate instrument of public policy. But it felt uneasy in this. Sometimes its authorities stipulated a penance for Christians killing anyone in war. After the battle of Hastings a council of bishops prescribed that every soldier in William the Conqueror's army should do penance for one year for every man he killed, and penance for forty days for every man he struck — even though the Pope had previously blessed William's expedition against England.

The Church encouraged restraint by propagating the "Truce of God", in which all fighting was to stop on Sundays and holy days. It also urged soldiers to respect the "Peace of God", which exempted monks, nuns, women, pilgrims, merchants and peasants from being attacked.

The acceptability of war was so dubious that Saint Thomas Aquinas in the thirteenth century wrote about it under the heading "Vices Opposed to Charity." He tried to show that fighting a war was not always a sin. "In order for a war to be just, three things are necessary. First, the authority of the sovereign by whose command the war is to be waged. . . . Secondly, a just cause is required, namely that those who are attacked, should be attacked because they deserve it on account of some fault. . . . Thirdly, it is necessary that the belligerents should have a rightful intention, so that they intend the advancement of good, or the avoidance of evil" (Summa Theologica, II-II, 40, I).

Later Dominican and Jesuit theologians, notably Francisco de Vitoria, Francisco Suarez, and Thomas de Vio Cajetan, amplified Aquinas' succinct formulation with three more conditions: (4) a war must be fought in the proper manner, without destruction of *the innocent (the principle of non-combatant immunity); (5) the punishment for injustice must not exceed the guilt, that is, the destruction caused by war must not be greater than the offense which provoked it (the principle of proportionality); and, finally, (6) war must be fought only as the last resort, after every other effort has been made to solve the dispute peaceably. These six conditions came to be accepted as the core of the Just War Theory. If all of them were fulfilled in a particular war, it would be morally right for a Christian to take part. These conditions became the framework within which the Church thought it could reconcile the Christian law of love with the practical necessity of war.*

The restraint imposed by Christ's command to turn the other cheek and to love one's enemies was completely relaxed during the Crusades. Christian soldiers had found an enemy on whom they could let loose the full fury of their desires. Those against whom they were fighting were infidels, enemies of God. The Crusades were a Holy War, and because the Crusaders were confident that God was unequivocally on their side, they didn't hold back. The Crusades remain one of the most severe blots on the history of the Christian Church.

The Gospel restraint was also frequently relaxed in practice, if not in theory, as the Church all too often yielded to the rising tide of modern nationalism. Clergy blessed the guns on both sides as Christians fought one another in nineteenth and twentieth century Europe. The Church's voice of peace had been largely hushed.

In recent years Church leaders have spoken out more strongly against war. Pope John XXIII stated in his encyclical Pacem in Terris, *in 1963, "In this age which boasts of its atomic power, it no longer makes sense to maintain that war is a fit instrument with which to repair the violation of justice." The Second Vatican Council in 1965 placed the Roman Catholic bishops of the world on record against some measures which had become common practice by the end of World War II: "Any act of war aimed indiscriminately at the destruction of entire cities or of extensive areas along with their population is a crime against God and man himself. It merits unequivocal and unhesitating condemnation" (The Church in the* Modern World, *Part II, Chap. 5, n.80).*

The words of Pope Paul VI to the United Nations in the fall of the same year showed the tension that has characterized the Church's attitude toward war over the centuries. On the one hand he declared, with beautiful simplicity, "If you wish to be brothers, let the arms fall from your hands. One cannot love while holding offensive arms." But, he continued, "As long as man remains that weak, changeable and even wicked being that he often shows himself to be, defensive arms will, unfortunately, be necessary." Pope Paul could not bring himself to a clear and complete condemnation of war. Since all modern nations characterize their armaments as defensive, he

10

left the door open for their use. Again the Church seemed to compromise.

Because of Vietnam, many Americans in the 1960's came to a new awareness of the horror of war. A spirit of revulsion began to spread through the Church's ranks. If bishops have failed to condemn their nations' wars, other members of the Church are now forcefully voicing their opposition. Roman Catholics have protested, burned draft files, and have been arrested for opposing war policies. Some, like the Berrigan brothers, are accused with great national publicity of conspiracy against the government.

II

The same kind of disgust welled up in Europe after the bloodbath of World War I. Many concerned people turned away from the traditional Christian acquiescence in war, and expressed their concern openly. The Church and War, written in the 1920's by a German theologian, Franziscus Stratmann, expressed for that decade the spirit that has enlarged the ranks of the peace movement around the world in the 1960's and 70's. Father Stratmann, born in 1883 and ordained a Roman Catholic priest of the Dominican Order in 1912, had been chaplain to the Catholic students at the University of Berlin during the first World War. Seeing many of his best students march vigorously off to fight and return bloodied, crippled or dead impelled him to devote his life to the cause of peace. Out of the Roman Catholic theological tradition he succeeded in formulating an anti-war position that appealed to tens of thousands of his fellow countrymen. Under Father Stratmann's leadership the Friedensbund deutscher Katholiken *(German Catholic Peace Union), which he had founded in Berlin, grew to a membership of over 40,000 persons throughout Germany. Because of his outspoken opposition to militaristic nationalism he was one of the first Catholic priests to be arrested by the Gestapo when Hitler came to power in 1933, and was imprisoned for several months in Berlin, Spandau and Frankfurt without trial. When he was released his Dominican superiors quickly removed him from Germany and assigned him to the relatively safe — and dull — work of hearing confessions at the basilica of Saint Mary Major in Rome.*

After five years of this kind of exile Father Stratmann moved back closer to the events that were shaping history. He took up residence in the Dominican monastery in Venlo in Holland in 1938, and began actively working to assist those victims of Nazi persecution who could escape from Germany. Early in 1940 the Nazi government revoked his German citizenship, and again made him a prime target for arrest when Holland fell in May to the German army. This time Father Stratmann managed to elude the Gestapo when he found a hiding place in a convent of Belgian Dominican nuns in Antwerp. In

INTRODUCTION

*gratitude for the great risks the nuns took for five years in concealing him Father Stratmann later wrote a book about the inspiring work they were doing with young troubled girls (*Neither Will I Condemn Thee, London, Blackfriars, 1955*).*

The Dominican seminary in Walberberg served as his home base when in 1947 he returned to Germany to resume his work for peace. His final book, War and Christianity Today *(Westminster, Newman, 1956), which takes up the problems posed by a world armed with nuclear weapons, argues forcefully for Christian conscientious objection to war.*

But Father Stratmann was never an absolute pacifist. His thinking developed out of the traditional Just War position which the Catholic Church has maintained for centuries. His books penetratingly analyzed the phenomenon of modern war, and his conclusion was that war fought with the weapons and tactics used in this century cannot be justified by traditional theological norms.

The Church and War, *which articulated the foundations of his thinking, remains his basic book. The freshly remembered First World War, then the horrible example of all modern international conflict, served as the focal point for his analysis. With the exception of Aquinas' first condition for a just war, that it must be declared by the sovereign authority, he found that all of the six major conditions mentioned previously were violated in World War I. He described the violations in detail.*

13

INTRODUCTION

Father Stratmann explained how the disputes among nations which caused the World War had tangled roots in history, making it extremely difficult to evaluate the issues clearly enough. There was considerable doubt about who was right and who was wrong. This doubt, he said, makes it impossible to determine for certain the grounds for what Aquinas stated as the second condition, the just cause, "Namely that those who are attacked, should be attacked because they deserve it on account of some fault." Where a significant doubt exists in an area of such importance, moral principles insist that no punitive action be undertaken.

He described how the savage campaigns of World War I were accompanied by a rise of greed and lust and hatred in those who were fighting, contradicting Aquinas' third conditions for a just war, "that the belligerents should have a rightful intention."

A considerable part of The Church and War *was devoted to explaining how the advanced instruments of killing used by both sides — machine guns, poison gas, bombs — inevitably caused the death of non-combatants. Women, children, and men who had not gone into military service, or who were conscripted against their will, fell victim to these weapons. Such indiscriminate killing is directly contrary to the fourth of the six central principles of a just war, that the innocent be spared.*

The kind of war Father Stratmann knew involved the destruction of lives, homes, and cities, causing agonies which far exceeded the injustice which provoked it in the first place. He argued that the fifth condition, that of proportionality, was not fulfilled. The suffering was too great. Modern wars are clearly not fought after all diplomatic efforts and attempts at arbitration have been tried. The sixth major condition for a just war, that it be launched only as a last resort, is not met.

Because modern war cannot fulfill the conditions for a just war it is wrong, immoral and sinful. The Church should do everything possible to prevent it in the future. The Church and War *was a fine example of theological thought put in the service of peace.*

Between the two World Wars Father Stratmann was recognized as one of the leading Roman Catholic theologians of peace. Others were as knowledgeable and sometimes more detailed in their presentation of the Just War tradition (e.g., A. Vanderpol, La Doctrine Scholastique du Droit de la Guerre, *Paris, 1919, and R. Regout,* La Doctrine de la Guerre Juste de Saint Augustin à Nos Jours, *Paris, 1935), but Father Stratmann was almost alone in carrying this tradition to its logical conclusion of modern war's indefensibility. The* Catholic Worker, *which in the 1930's had been the dominant Catholic voice of pacifism in the United States, provided a forum for his ideas before as well as after the second World War.*

The value of The Church and War *is not diminished by some of Father Stratmann's expressions which, after Vatican II, seem naïve and triumphalistic. He* wrote, in praise of the Church, that it brought to the world "new ideals, new standards of duty, new manners, new laws. Men of all races and of all times, civilized and barbarous, have submitted to her. No other institution in the world could accomplish what she has done" (pp. 22-23). His words are a bit extravagant, needing perhaps a balancing sentence to present a more sober view of the Church's effect on the world. The idealistic picture he constantly paints of the Church does not interfere with the fundamental thrust of his work, which is to declare that war now and in the future is intolerable.

Some passages in The Church and War sound ironical today. "The whole character of war has changed since the advent of the machine gun. Now men are shot down in hordes by an enemy they cannot see and who cannot see them" (p. 28). Although the machine gun and the poison gas of World War I seemed to concerned people in the 1920's to be the ultimate weapons of their time, they are insignificant in comparison to the ultimate weapons of the 1970's. Governments now possess — and use — high altitude bombers which set fire to square miles of land, atomic bombs which destroy entire cities, jellied gasoline which sticks to the flesh as it burns, and chemicals capable of rapidly and thoroughly destroying all forms of life.

War has become so terrible that it should no longer be allowed to happen. Father Stratmann recalled the hope of one English bishop that if the nineteenth century did away with slavery, the twentieth century could do away with war (p. 50). He urged that Church leaders take significant steps to prevent war. Priests and ministers can make clear to young men that refusing military service is in accord with the highest Christian principles. The Pope should forbid Catholics to participate in war under penalty of excommunication, the same way they are now excommunicated if they take part in a duel (p. 175). The Church, he said, must take the lead in forming a community of nations and in spreading a feeling of international brotherhood among peoples of different races and social classes.

Standing squarely in the way of world peace is the exaggerated spirit of nationalism inherent in the slogan "my country, right or wrong" (p. 193). Nations today can be what Paul Tillich called idols. Father Stratmann thought this metaphor appropriate, since nations often receive allegiance ahead of God (p. 189). They demand the ultimate concern of their citizens. But because their posture is often if not predominantly selfish and hostile to others, the ultimate concern which they demand is wrongly given. Total commitment must extend to all mankind.

Besides the special love which a person will feel for his family and for those closest to him, Father Stratmann wrote, "it is a duty to feel a strong and real love for all mankind. This is the Christian law which looks upon everyone as our neighbor, even as *our brother in Christ" (p. 200). Love of one's nation can easily hinder the universal love a Christian is urged to have.*

Father Stratmann's conclusion was unequivocal: "We must give up trying to square the spirit of modern war with the Spirit of Christ. We must acknowledge that they can no more amalgamate than can fire and water" (p. 42). His theological reasoning, however, led him to uphold the abstract possibility of a just war, even though he strongly denies that any concrete war in the modern world can be justified. Theoretically, he said, a nation can go to war in self defense to correct an injustice done to it. The Just War Theory assumes that nations have the same rights to life, dignity and property as have individual persons, and consequently can legitimately defend themselves when these rights are violated.

Some observations are in order. A nation has no independent life of its own. It is nothing more than a group of people who live within common geographic boundaries, share many of the same ideals and cultural values, and are governed by the same authority. A nation consists entirely of its own citizens, nothing more. Nations as groupings of people were not created equal, only their individual members were. A nation as such has no God-given right to its territory, or even to its existence, where these interfere with human development. It is not nations, but their citizens who have rights to life, dignity and property, provided that their dignity is not falsely assumed at the expense of others' degradation, and provided that their property is not stolen or otherwise unjustly appropriated. It is not nations but their citizens, therefore, who have the right of self-defense. War as the act of a nation has to be carefully rethought, particularly in light of the spirit of nationalism which has dominated the world scene for several centuries, and which calls for citizens to subordinate their highest values of justice and brotherhood to the interests of the nation.

III

We are today faced with the heart of the problem. Which comes first, the nation or mankind? The widespread revulsion following World War I did not stop the swelling of nationalistic pride which led to even more horrible destruction a little more than two decades later. The frenzied end of the second world catastrophe in the nuclear burning of hundreds of thousands of civilians, far worse than anything seen previously, left the world numbed. The world wanted no more war after 1918, but in 1939 it plunged in again. By 1945 something had happened to the world's conscience. Massive destruction of cities with their populations became an accepted tactic in achieving the goals of a government.

The world feared Hitler and the criminals who dominated Nazi Germany when it learned they were *insensitive to human life, when it learned that they coldly murdered millions of people. But by 1945 the leaders of England, Russia and the United States were themselves ordering hundreds of thousands of people killed by bombing, and they have established a military system which is prepared to carry out similar orders right now on a far larger scale.*

Still, there are hopeful signs in the air. More and more people around the world are coming to recognize the limitations of their national interest. A trans-national spirit is rising, made possible by an intensifying web of communications and the realization that resources are available to meet the common aspirations of mankind. Nationalistic sentiments are coming to be viewed as shortsighted and harmful. If wars are based on national interests, then a strong trans-national spirit will eventually be an effective antidote.

Besides a disenchantment with nationalism and the realization of war's essential inhumanity, an appreciation of every person's fundamental right to life seems to be spreading. There is a renewed respect for the commandment, "Thou shalt not kill." More people are coming to question the fundamental breakdown of the prohibition against killing, and are trying to come to grips with the tendency to violence that seems to be a part of the human makeup. Our brightest hope for the future rests on this slowly growing appreciation of the beauty of human lives. The Christian Churches can help propagate this spirit if, in the name of their traditional respect for human life, they will speak out against war with the same intensity that they have shown on occasions against slavery, alcohol and abortion.

To this day, the Catholic Worker *continues to carry on a courageous pacifist stand, sometimes alone among Catholic voices in the United States. When Catholic spokesmen were contributing to the patriotic fervor for military service during World War II (for a particularly blatant example see* The Catholic at War, *by Msgr. J.J. Burke, New York, 1942), the* Catholic Worker *people were organizing an Association of Catholic Conscientious Objectors. In the rigid national security atmosphere of the 1950's which saw Catholic theologians like Father John Courtney Murray cautiously spelling out the conditions under which nuclear weapons could be used in a morally acceptable way (cf. his article "Remarks on the Moral Problem of War" in* Theological Studies, March, 1959), *Dorothy Day and her friends were being arrested for refusing to participate in civil defense drills. Her publication spoke out clearly and forcefully against the Vietnam War when most other American Catholics were still giving unquestioned assent to their government's actions.*

The Catholic Worker *movement in 1964 was directly responsible for one of the two presently existing American Catholic organizations for peace, the Catholic Peace Fellowship, which is affiliated with the interdenominational Fellowship of Recon-*

ciliation. The other is the Division of World Justice and Peace, the American Catholic bishops' counter-part to the Vatican's Pontifical Commission on Justice and Peace. As the official voice of the U.S. Catholic hierarchy on the subject of peace it succeeds the Catholic Association for International Peace, which served this function from 1926 until it was formally discontinued in 1968.

The pacifist position, which Father Stratmann reached by applying the Just War tradition to the actual condition of war in the twentieth century, is carried on vigorously by a number of writers today. Before he died Thomas Merton had developed his pacifist position from the Gospels and the writings of Gandhi (cf., for example, his Faith and Violence, *Notre Dame, 1968). James Douglass (especially in* The Non-Violent Cross, *New York, Macmillan, 1966) has shown how the Just War tradition no longer applies in the nuclear age. Gordon Zahn brings his sociological expertise to bear on the problems of war (e.g.,* German Catholics and Hitler's Wars, *New York, Dutton, 1969), and has worked out a theory of national defense based on non-violent techniques (*An Alternative to War, *Council on Religion and International Affairs, 1963). These three writers are the most outstanding of many Catholics who are joining other members of the religious community in calling for an end to war and the establishment of a just international order.*

The Second Vatican Council urged men of good

INTRODUCTION

will to evaluate war with an entirely new attitude, to approach the whole question with a different mind-set. The Just War Theory, if it ever applied to conditions in the world outside the cloistered minds of scholastic theologians, seems utterly and hopelessly obsolete today.

There remain only two positions. One attempts to justify war in defense of human values, while allowing the use of weapons which destroy human values. The other refuses participation in wars because they are inhuman, and works to spread the spirit of non-violence throughout the world.

Gerard A. Vanderhaar
Christian Brothers College
Memphis, Tenn.
July 25, 1971

THE CHURCH AND WAR
A CATHOLIC STUDY

THE
CHURCH AND WAR
A Catholic Study

BY

FRANZISKUS STRATMANN, O.P.

LONDON:
SHEED AND WARD
31 PATERNOSTER ROW, E.C.4.

Nihil Obstat
THOMAS McLAUGHLIN, S.T.D.
CENSOR DEPUTATUS

Imprimatur
EDM: CAN: SURMONT
VIC. GEN.

WESTMONASTERII,
die 11 Octobris 1928

Printed in Great Britain by The Crypt House Press Limited
Gloucester and London

CONTENTS

INTRODUCTION vii

I. THE MYSTICAL BODY OF CHRIST
A. Dogma 17
B. Ethics 22

II. WAR AND THE MYSTICAL BODY
A. The Destruction of Natural
   Foundations 31
B. The Moral Destruction 35
C. War and Missionary Work ... 41

III. THE METAPHYSICAL AND MORAL PROBLEM
A. The Necessity of War 47
B. Just and Unjust War
   (1) In the Natural Law 52
   (2) In Revelation
      (a) In the Old Testament ... 80
      (b) In the New Testament ... 84

v

IV. THEORIES OF PEACE
    A. IN THE PAST
        (1) OUTSIDE THE CHURCH 95
        (2) WITHIN THE CHURCH 110
    B. IN THE PRESENT
        (1) OUTSIDE THE CHURCH 134
        (a) Classic Pacifism 135
        (b) Religious Pacifism 143
        (c) Young Pacifism 150
        (2) WITHIN THE CHURCH 158

V. PATRIOTISM 179

VI. LOVE OF MANKIND 199

VII. PROSPECT AND RETROSPECT ... 207

INTRODUCTION

As month and year succeeded one another and the World War raged with increasing fury, the feeling and hope grew that this must indeed be " the war to end war," that out of this unparalleled upheaval a new dispensation would be born, that war would be seen to be not only foolish but immoral, and that its immorality and horror would outweigh the idealism with which the self sacrifice and loyalty and heroism of many thousands had clothed it. And although, alas, the standpoint of the life of nations is not so quickly altered, yet the fact remains that we are at a turning point in history. The outlines are not yet quite sharply defined, just as night and day shade off into one another through the transition stage of twilight. In our transition stage we are emerging from the Renaissance, which was the age of individualism, both in culture and religion. It set the individual free, which might have had no evil results if it had not brought with it the great religious schism and the blow aimed at the Church's unity.

This spirit has had four hundred years in which to work itself out. The individualising, as well as the isolating, of men and peoples and states has gone on increasing. On the plane of politics this individualism developed in the last hundred years into nationalism, which has resulted in the World War, and even the war was not in vain if it showed us that the corporate life of Europe was being destroyed by individualism and its consequences.

And since then have we not seen much the same ? Not so clearly as during the war, when there was one life of fellowship common to a whole nation—even to the group of nations in alliance.

These national blocks have dissolved, especially in the conquered countries which were too weakened to have the strength to support a common experience. And yet there is a common after-war *experience* which is no longer national but super-national—a longing for unity which must develop into a real League of Nations. This ideal is still very small, very immature, but it exists and the most hopeful sign of this recognition of the solidarity of the race is the awakening of the sense of religious fellowship. What else do the strivings for reunion signify ? and who can deny the ever increasing moral authority of the Father of Christendom ?

This new time of faith and world-wide organisation is not yet. The time of transition is nothing but an advent, a time of longing and of hope, and like the Church's Advent, it must be a time of self-examination and penance. The world's Advent must rest on the acknowledgment of the world's guilt. The question of bloodguilt must be answered, not before the court of the politician, but before the high court of history, of humanity, of conscience, of God. It is amazing how a Christian faced with this question of guilt can throw all principle to the winds—how he will consider any answer unfavourable to his own country as treason, and how superficially he will pass over this deeply important matter. In this modern shrinking from recognition and confession of fault and in the abuse of those who have the courage to put their finger on these open wounds and sins, we see clearly how far we have fallen below the spirit of Christianity in the middle ages.

What in the Church are virtues—humility, penitence, confession—in the market place of social and political life are a disgrace. The Renaissance led to the pagan worship of the State, but before the Renaissance such a tearing in two of religion and conscience would have been impossible. In those days the preacher, backed by the moral authority of the Church, could call political crimes by their true names and bring them to judgment. To-day woe betide him who, now the war is ended, would call men to a penitential procession in acknowledgment not of private sins but of the sins of the state.

Processions may not be the form which penances take to-day—the spoken and written word may take their place : but the thing itself must be there and it must begin with the acknowledgment of national guilt. The teachers and leaders of the people must undertake a public examination of conscience, and the young especially must be led to be humble instead of overbearing. But as things are to-day, a national acknowledgment of guilt would be considered worse than the guilt itself. If this attitude were universal there would be no Advent ; but the light is beginning to break through in many places, and this is the first sign of improvement.

Self-knowledge in itself is not improvement but only the first step towards it, and it is quite true that the uncovering of social wounds and reckless self-criticism may become both unhealthy and immoral ; but short of such excess it is better than the dead level of crystallised custom and self-complacency. Paul Ludwig Landsberg, in his most thoughtful book, *Der Welt des Mittelalters und wir* (*The world of the middle ages and ourselves*), divides history into three periods : 1. *Order* united to God. 2. Purely conventional hide-bound *Custom* and, as its result : 3. *Anarchy* which breaks away both from order and custom. Anarchy has that amount of good in it that it is an awakening from stupor and a yearning after what is new and better.

To-day the world lives in this state of anarchy. We have to go back to the middle ages to find the state of order united to God. Before the war conventional custom was widespread. In the war anarchy broke loose and to many this, and the German Revolution which followed, seemed to herald a return to order, to harmony with the whole, to submission to those higher ideals which must rule once more if the world and mankind are to come to their senses and to know their happiness again.

After self-knowledge the second thing that leads to improvement is belief in oneself, in the possibility of improvement. This saves us from pessimism, from Judas Iscariot's sin of despair. The triumph of Christianity would have been impossible if prophets, saints and martyrs filled with undying hope and living more in the future than in the present had not held fast against the conventionality of Judaism and the anarchy of paganism.

So it must be to-day. What is lost? Only what we and God surrender. Till that happens all may yet be won—even the past. The past is still in flux and may look in time very different from what it looks to-day. The World War may yet be won for the whole world.

If a great breakwater is destroyed, the river's course is altered in its higher reaches as well as in its forward course. We must look back, acknowledge our guilt and ask pardon of God and man ; we must look forward resolved to avoid our former faults. That would be a past and a future deliverance, a new Advent for the world.

The universal Church, as no one else, is called to the work of restoring the world. The Church, the kingdom of God, " is like unto leaven which a woman took and hid in three measures of meal that the whole might be leavened." The meal, the world, is in opposition, is refractory and so are many who belong to the Church. The Church itself contains both the divine and the human element, and the divine does not seem to prevail. The great, wonderful, inspiring power is the soul of the Church, the Holy Ghost, who dwells in the mystical Body and trains numberless members in marvellous strength and beauty, but leaves others to themselves so that through their own fault they become weak and sickly and even die, thus becoming a burden and torment to the whole Body. That is why the Church annoys so many people. They under-value her divine element and over-estimate her human. They think only of her educative power and forget her divinity, which is of course far the greater—her power to save, to sow the seed of holy living, to tend and watch over her mystic life which, hidden from the world, at last leads silently from earth to heaven. If the Church gave the world no more than this, she would still be its most precious treasure.

We Catholics know that the idea of the Church cannot *really* suffer through insufficient appreciation, but it is our duty to help on the work to the limit of our power, and we must judge ourselves more severely than the world judges us : for God will judge us too.

Our aim in this book is to learn how we can bring the world out of anarchy to order, how we can answer the call for help even if it comes to us in the form of curses, how we can heal the special wound from which our world to-day is suffering : that wildest form of anarchy which is war. The Christian attitude to war is severely criticised by socialism all the world over.

Even from India and China comes the same complaint ; and though there may be much exaggeration, is it wise or humble to treat these criticisms with contempt ? If there is only the smallest germ of truth in them, are we not bound to listen and to search our conscience ? If we do not, will not Christ accuse us ?   Scheler truly says that to speak of the bankruptcy of Christendom would only be true if Christianity had been the pre-ponderating and leading force in Europe.   Still this is far from satisfactory.

Meanwhile the work is too great for the masses. The masses feel the necessity of a great reaction, but they have not the strength to react.   Times of transition are times for a leader even in the Church.

Paul Landsberg gives us a typical representation for each of his three periods.   The ideal of *Order* is the priest, of conventional, mechanical *Custom* the religious official, of the restless fearful *Anarchy* the prophet.

It is a blessed fact that in the movement with which we are concerned (towards a new and better state of things), the Catholic movement towards the world's peace working itself out from anarchy and from the folly of the nations, the prophet should be he who held the highest office in the Church, Pope Benedict XV. It is true that many of his own children have mis-understood and misrepresented him.   His enemies have been those of his own house, but we must look beyond all this.   " If a man put his hand to the plough and turn back he is not worthy of the Kingdom of God."   The plough is the sword of the Spirit which Christ gives into the hands of His followers that with Him they may overcome all opposition.   But the kingdom to be won is God's kingdom of peace.   It must be created first in the Church and then through the Church in the world.   May the time be not so far off, for come it will ; and even if there are a thousand hindrances, a thousand wars, the Church must still preach peace more and more strongly, and even if she were to fail (and who can believe that possible ?) she could still declare before God and man *Dixi et salvavi animam meam*—I have spoken, I have delivered my soul and my conscience.

CHAPTER I
THE MYSTICAL BODY OF CHRIST
A. DOGMA
B. ETHICS

THE CHURCH AND WAR

THE MYSTICAL BODY OF CHRIST

A. DOGMA

IN 1922 appeared Romano Guardini's book, *The Mind of the Church*. It began with the phrase, " A religious event of indescribable importance has taken place : the Church is awakening in Souls."

This astonishing statement does not, of course, mean that the Church has hitherto never been awake. It refers to the state of slumber in the very near past—men to-day are in a more trusting attitude to the Church than they were. And why ? Because the age we have just left behind was an age of excessive *individualism* and the new age is one of *solidarity*. In the last century, great stress was laid on personality and the Church, with her common life, common truth, common moral was looked upon as the enemy of personality.

Personality is not forgotten to-day, but the interests of the community have come to the front.

And so the Church awakes in souls. Men remember that she is the ideal community—old as time and still ever new, deep and still crystal clear.

The Church, indeed, has another side. She is an

organisation, a Society under law, and this is the side the world mostly sees. Holy Scripture, tradition and history all testify to this truth. Scripture speaks of the Church as the City, the House, the Kingdom. All images of a visible Society. The Græco-Latin word *Ecclesia* meant originally some great secular, political assembly of people. St. Paul was the first to use this idea for a religious crowd, or assembly of the faithful, and it is noteworthy that he never speaks simply of the *Ecclesia*, but always of the *Ecclesia of God*.

Thus St. Paul gives us a new idea which lifts the Church above all the things of the world and which is better understood the more the spirit of solidarity grows : the idea of the deepest fellowship in the mystical Body of Christ.

The idea that men were one Body was not new. The Pagan world had looked upon the state, upon the whole *Kosmos*, as one, and had realised that it was Love, as in the Christian idea, that bound this body together. We see this in concrete form in the Old Testament. The whole nation of Israel was spoken of as one—Israel, the Servant of Jehovah, the Son of God. Israel was spoken to as *thou*, not *you*. But the fellowship of the New Testament surpasses that of Paganism or Judaism as Heaven surpasses earth, for in this fellowship of God and Man it is not I and thou, but one body, of their Christian Body, the God-Made-Man is a member —the greatest member, their Head.

Before we examine the Church further in her mystical, invisible character, let us consider her once more on her visible side. The most common image under which she is represented, and the best understood by Catholics and non-Catholics alike—is the house built upon the rock. This image stirs in us a feeling of veneration for its age and of astonishment at its strength and beauty. But it can also arouse a sense of fear and awe—even a sense of repulsion from the bare high walls and the deep moats which seem to make approach so difficult.

Thus on the one hand we have the plain description of the Church as a visible company and fellowship, and on the other an emphatic assertion of the Divine Invisible Head of this remarkable organisation.

The acknowledgment of the inner Being of the Church is truly an act of Faith. We can grasp her external side with our intellect and with our senses : but *Credo Ecclesiam*. The Church is a mystery of the Faith.

First the. Church is the visible fellowship of the Faithful, built by Christ on the rock of Peter and founded on the Apostles and Prophets.

Secondly, the faithful, through the new birth of Baptism, are united to Christ, the head of the Body. They all confess the same Creed, use the same means of Grace, follow the same laws and precepts, in order, under the guidance of the Holy Ghost, to show forth the Kingdom of God on earth and to obtain eternal Life.

The *Credo* is of value as regards our attitude to the visible Church, as it gives us in two respects a different outlook from the purely national. When once we acknowledge that both in the past and in the present the Roman Catholic Church, founded by Christ upon the rock which is Peter, is the only true Church, we suppose a supernatural Faith in the promise of Christ and in the uninterrupted guidance of the Holy Ghost in the Church. We see too with overwhelming clearness that the line of development is unbroken from Christ through Peter to the present Pope, and that the difference between then and to-day is only the difference between the seed and the tree which has grown out of it. This knowledge not only shows us the historical phenomenon and compels us to exclaim *Scio*, I know, I see ; it leads us further, even to the very threshold of this secret, where, moved by grace, we cry : *Credo*, I believe.

The visible Church was not built before the invisible but the faithful—each one the temple of the Holy Ghost—are the living stones built upon the foundation of Apostles and Prophets and Christ Himself the chief corner stone, in whom the whole building is joined together and grows into a holy Temple (Eph. II., 20–21) : the visible Church is not only a result of the Faith but also its work and witness. We believe because the Church is there, and the Church is there because we believe. The visible and invisible are thus so intermixed that we bow before the *Credo Ecclesiam* and acknowledge even the visible Church to be a reality to be grasped even more by our mystical sense than as a historical phenomenon.

When one part of the family suffers, the other part suffers with it. We help one another in every condition of life. But the Church is more than a moral or legal personality. Her oneness with Christ the Head and with Christians as Members, rests on the real and continuous influx of supernatural life from the Head to the Members. Grace—the *gratia capitis*—is, according to St. Peter (2. I., 4), a partaking of the Divine Nature. Thus fellowship goes far beyond a mere fellowship of thought or teaching or imitation or service. It is such a fullness of living fellowship that Christ can say, " I am the vine—ye are the branches," and St. Paul, " I live and yet not I but Christ lives in me."

St. Paul gives us another illustration of the union of Christ and the Church, i.e. the union of man and wife. The persons are distinct but their union is so close that they are not only morally but physically one. This gives us a very different idea of the Church from the popular Protestant or superficial Catholic idea. For such the Church is only a society which meets to study Christ as the Goethe Society meets to study Goethe. As the Goethe Society stands to Goethe so stands the Church of the Liberal Christian to Christ. It honours, loves and follows Him as the Goethe Society does Goethe. The Liberal Church is a religious society for the cultivation of a liberal religious outlook, a purely human association. The Catholic Church is a religious Society for the cultivation of the Catholic outlook ; but she is far more—she is a Divine and human Fellowship. The God-Man is not only the historic Head of His Church Who, since His Ascension watches over and leads Her ; but according to Catholic teaching the God-Man remains ever with man on earth, one with them, their *chiefest* Member, their Head, organically and spiritually one with them.

And here we see the supernatural origin of the Church. It is not, like other societies, the coming together of many individuals. The Church grows from Christ as Head, not from men, the members. Men do not weld the Church together, Christ does this (Eph. IV., 16), and thus the Body, composed of the Baptized members who are united to Christ as closely as the parts of a body to the head, becomes both Divine and human. The Church is a Divine and human organism. Really to grasp the idea of the whole Mystical Body of Christ, we must look beyond this world to Heaven. There is one Head, the Glorified Christ. And there is the body —one body—containing as cells, so to say, not only the members of the Church on earth, but all the blessed in Heaven and the suffering in Purgatory. It is the physical fact that one part of a body *in union with the head* can help another : that explains the Catholic practice of prayers to the Saints and prayers *for* the dead in Purgatory. So we are no more strangers and foreigners, but fellow-citizens with the Saints and of the household of God (Eph. II., 19).

B. ETHICS.

In the Epistle to the Ephesians we find that celebrated word, *Omnia instaurare in Christo*, "restore all in Christ" (Eph. I., 10). A better translation of ἀνακεφαλαιώσασθαι τὰ πάντα ἐν τῷ Χριστῷ is "to give to all a Head in Christ," or "to unite again under one Head." But the sense is the same. If Christ is the Head, the Means, the End of everything, He must be acknowledged as such by all. Everything must be under Him and become more completely His. A practical result is the demand for the growth of His Kingdom in breadth and depth. We must consider the circumference of the status of this kingdom. Who belongs to it? Who only outwardly, who inwardly, who both outwardly and inwardly?

We distinguish between the Body and the Soul of the Church. By the Body, we do not mean here the mystical Body of Christ, but the external corporate Body of the Church. To this, all properly baptized Christians belong—all at least who have not formally cut themselves off from the Roman Catholic Church. There are about 1,700 million people in the world of whom some 316 million are Catholics.

Is this, as the result of 1900 years of Christianity, satisfactory or the reverse? It is both. To have won so many to the Church is certainly tremendous—no other religion has done as much. And as the Roman Catholic Church is spread over the whole world, she can truly be called the Universal Church.

What this purely external Catholicism has done for the world must be clear to anyone who considers her culture and the supernatural greatness of her ideals. This Church brought with her new ideals, new standards of duty, new manners, new laws. Men of all races and of all times, civilised and barbarous, have submitted to her. No other institution in the world could accomplish what she has done. On the other hand, we must be saddened when we think how many millions are either almost or completely uninfluenced by the Catholic Church.

First there are non-Catholics who do not belong to the Body of the Church at all. Still, according to Catholic teaching, without their membership they may be united to the Soul of the Church and have the Spirit of Christ and be united to Him, enjoy His Supernatural Grace and be saved. Such souls are inwardly Catholic and the Dogma that outside the Church there is no Salvation is untouched, for it applies to the Soul of the Church, but their position outside the Body of the Church, without her teaching and her means of Grace, is full of danger and the word of St. Augustine about non-Catholics is full of warning. " Wilt thou live by the Spirit of Jesus Christ ? Then be in the Body of Jesus Christ. Does *my* body by chance live by *thy* Spirit ? My body lives by my Spirit and thine by thy Spirit." The living " by my Spirit," as pupil and disciple without bodily oneness is possible, but how much weaker must that union be without the corporal oneness. True oneness can only be when body and soul make one person. So that there can only be complete oneness with Christ when we belong not only to His Soul, but also to His Body, which is the Church.

It is also possible to belong to the Body of the Church and not to the Soul. A person may be outwardly a Catholic, but may lack the inner Spirit. He has the name, but he is dead. He is indeed a member of the Body, but the supernatural life of Grace which comes from Christ the Head does not flow through him, only his faith keeps him still united to the Body. God only knows how many Catholics are in this state—

hanging between Spiritual life and death—yet it is not
a hopeless state because by virtue of their Membership
in the Church their return to the fulness of Spiritual
life is always easy.

There is another Spiritual condition with which this
book has specially to deal. Many Catholics fulfil all
their obligations as Members of the Body of Christ
and still leave much to be desired in their lives. There
are many Catholics, very correct—unimpeachable in
their Faith, yet lacking in one thing which Membership
with Christ should bring and that is the Spirit of Christ.
They settle themselves comfortably in the *House* of
the Church, but they do not breathe the Life of the
Body of the Church, which is much more important.
The figure of the Church as the House built on the
rock is easier to accept than that of the Body, for in a
large house men of very varying parties and tastes can
live and not come up against one another. Not so in
the Church as the Body. The cells and organs and
members of one Body cannot ignore each other. If they
do, the whole Body suffers. Too many Catholics fulfil
their obligations as to Mass and the other precepts of
the Church, bring up their children as Catholics, and
are most exact and correct. With their body and soul
they accept the Church as a well-ordered house, but
what about the Church as the Mystical Body of Christ?
To be a Catholic means nothing less than to be one
with all fellow-Christians in will and love and deed and
sacrifice, just as all the Members of the Body are one
with each other and with the Head.

He is the Christian who follows Christ even if not
in acts of heroism yet in the things of daily life, for it
is just in these elementary things of daily life that we
miss, in these external Catholics, the Spirit of Christ.
It is a reversal of Christian Ethics when more importance is given to the laws of the Church than to the

commands of the Gospels—when neglect of Sunday Mass is thought worse than outbreaks of pride and hate and revenge.

The greatest of all Catholic laws is that which follows from the Mystical Body of Christ : Love to the Head of this Body and to all its Members : " Neither Jew nor Greek . . . all one in Christ Jesus " (Gal. III., 28). Love and fellowship are the new specific likeness to Christ, greater than any natural sympathy, than any social or material interests.

Purely *natural* sympathy and interest have really nothing to do with the Christian Religion : they are no more than self-love, service of self, not love and service of God, love and service of Christ.

How far is the Christianity of to-day from the realisation of these ideals ! Two Heads of Christendom —two popes—have indeed done their duty without consideration of Nation or religion to the suffering Members of the human race, but the Body itself has been torn and rent in the most terrible manner through want of love and sympathy.

The universal Church seems to be like an enormous house divided into storeys and rooms in which nations and classes live separated, taking no heed of each other. In Russia thousands are dying of hunger, and in the United States we hear of the most terrible waste, of foodstuff being used as fuel because coal is so dear. No one can doubt that there is something wrong in the state of the world. A cloud of pessimism hangs over the nations, whilst Statesmen hurry from conference to conference. There is no feeling that man is responsible for his fellow-man, nation for nation. Nowadays a nation is simply so many millions of people. In the middle ages it was not so. It was recognised, perhaps subconsciously, that a family or a State was more than a given number of heads. It was a human biological entity—a fellowship. This consciousness found support and strength in the Christian conception of the common origin of mankind, of the Redemption of the whole world, of the one Universal Church. The teaching of the Mystical Body of Christ translated into the language of politics and Ethics is : Solidarity among nations and in national life.

If we are living in union with the Head, we have no other enemies than the enemies of Christ, and even then we will treat them as He treated them—we will try to overcome their evil with good.

CHAPTER II

WAR AND THE MYSTICAL BODY

A. The Destruction of Natural Foundations
B. The Moral Collapse
C. War and Missionary Work

Chapter II

WAR AND THE MYSTICAL BODY

Love is the *Vis connexiva*, the binding element in the Mystical Body, its fruit is that *unitas et pax*, union and peace, so often found together in the Liturgy. All want of Love, any breach of unity, is a destructive influence in the organism.

This want of Love and breach of unity reach their extreme point in War. Christ Himself suffers in each of His suffering Members (Col. I., 24), and war by which Christians suffer brings suffering to the Mystical Body of Christ, just as does any other suffering of Christians, even if there is no terrific upheaval. But what can we say when the war is a deadly struggle of Christian against Christian, of Member against Member?

There have been wars of Christians against non-Christians, Moors or Turks—truly sad enough, but these wars have been in defence of Christianity against the aggression of the unbeliever, not the paradox of war *within* the Mystical Body. But when Christian fights against Christian it is nothing short of suicide.

" Why," says Clement of Rome, writing to the Corinthians, " Why is there strife and anger, and dis-union and war among you? Have we not one God, one Christ? Is not one Holy Ghost poured out on us, have we not one calling in Christ? Why do the Members of Christ tear one another, why do we rise up against our own body in such madness; have we forgotten that we are all members one of another? "

29

In war all this is, of course, forgotten. Men have lost the consciousness that war is a destroying element in the Mystical Body of Christ. As for Christian consciousness to-day, we do not think of Christian fighting against Christian, but only of the citizens of one country fighting against those of another. War is looked at almost exclusively from the national point of view. No one denies that war, even within Christendom, must be looked at from such a point of view : that is the duty of the members of each nation ; to maintain and further their national interests : but it is an undeniable proof of the weakness of the Christian spirit when, as in the World War, the Christian is filled solely with national feeling, and the political collapse of the country is mourned much more bitterly than the moral and religious collapse of innumerable people. That is where the shame lies. Where are those for whom the bitterest sorrow of the War is that Christian fought against Christian and that an orgy of hatred and revenge was let loose because they behaved no differently from Pagans ?

How many Catholics were there, in the early days of the War, who suffered with Pius X., whose heart was broken by this spectacle ? How many were troubled by Benedict XV.'s cry of sorrow and distress ? The thoughts of the visible and the invisible Head of Christ's Mystical Body were of little importance. What mattered was that Head Quarters should announce " Two regiments were mowed down by our fire. A thousand enemy corpses lie in our lines." This would be read with beaming eyes ; healths would be drunk and a feast celebrated. It is sad enough that such things should give pleasure to the natural man : but he is ruled altogether by the struggle for existence, his strength consists in individual and collective egoism. It would be useless to lament over this spirit of fallen and therefore wounded humanity. What, in the name of a higher law, we deplore is the complete disappearance of the supernatural standard amongst those who are pledged to think on the highest plane.

A. THE DESTRUCTION OF NATURAL FOUNDATIONS.

We must next consider the devastation which war brings in the *natural* order to the foundation of the Mystical Body of Christ, not only to supernatural, but also to natural thought.

Modern warfare is horrible and this even from the purely physical side—whole provinces trodden down, whole towns razed to the ground—no consideration for the noblest work of art or culture or religion—consecrated churches turned into stables—the sight of a battlefield is quite indescribable—men turned into hyenas, not because they really have the nature of hyenas, but because that terrible Force which they have to serve dehumanises them so that they become mere machines of slaughter. No slaughter-house of animals can be compared with the battlefield of man. Exaggeration is impossible. It is all very well to say, " We don't speak of these things, *C'est la Guerre.*" No ! We must speak of this horror which has gone on with ever-growing fury for centuries, and which will only increase unless degraded mankind comes to itself and rises up against it. We cannot put the World War in the balance and weigh it in cold blood as if it were a bale of goods. Consider what harm to God and Man lies behind these figures. The statistics of the last war tell us that ten million men were killed, twenty to thirty million men were wounded, more than half a million houses destroyed. As we are given these statistics we are justified, are bound, to lay stress on the horror of it all, without respect for the romance of war. Here

humanitarianism and Christianity are one. The
Christian standard of course is not only utilitarian and
material, but moral, defined by the laws of God and
Christ, but at the same time we cannot, as has been
done, disregard the physical misery of war. I am at
liberty under certain circumstances to give up my
personal well-being, but I have no right to dispose of
that of other people. To prevent or to mitigate the
physical suffering of others is a moral duty. The
works of mercy stand high in the Christian category
and are even the manna of the soul : health for
Eternity : but bodily or spiritual wounds are not only
to be healed, they are to be prevented. It is therefore
a duty to truth and to love, to the past and to the
future, a work of mercy to the dead and to the living,
to expose the horrors of war in the strongest possible
light. Unfortunately such descriptions are mostly
found in pacifist and socialist literature. One reason
may be that in these circles there is far less sense than
among Christians of the tragedy of all earthly existence
or understanding of the preciousness of suffering. But
to belittle the physical horrors of war, as do so many
who bear the name of Christ, is to behave like the Priest
and Levite, and pass by on the other side.

Let us have the courage to face one of the numberless
tales of horror with human sympathy and Christian
pity—" A potato field covered with barbed wire—on
a fence hangs a man. He was shot and his foot is
shattered. The bleeding bones stick out of his shoe.
Another splinter has disembowelled him and his
entrails are hanging out : but he still lives. He had
tried to get free of the wire and his hand is torn and
bleeding ; he is too weak even to shake off the flies
which are settling on his wounds. One eye hangs out
with flies upon it. He does not even faint and he
cannot call out. One eye still moves and bubbles of

blood are between his lips as he draws his breath. There he hangs alive, hour after hour, in the burning sun, whilst the maggots are crawling in his wounds."*

This may be an extreme case. Others have something consecrated about them ; but on the whole there is little romance about modern warfare, and the young generation growing up since the war should have this drilled into them, so that they may not reproach us who know what war is. The idea of the romance of war may be dying, but it is not yet dead and we must show up its falseness. The best suffer in war. No doubt this suffering and death, if taken in the right spirit, is full of honour for the individual ; but how about the community ? Mankind in general ? and especially the Christian community ? Is it not shameful that such things should happen, and is it not the duty of all Christians to see that their children are spared them ? " Why," says Clement of Rome, " do we rend the members of Christ ? Why do we, in such folly, rise up against our own flesh ? "

The natural order has its place in the moral and religious outlook. The disturbance and upheaval to daily life caused by a great war are moral as well as material evil and a cause of sin when the destruction it brings with it falls on the bodies of men dedicated to God by their Baptism.

Now it is true that there is a good side to war as well as an evil, both in the material and the moral order. The question is whether the good so outweighs the evil as to justify the making of war. " But war has its honour, it rules man's fate." The quotation from *The Bride of Messina* is taken by Max Scheler as the motto of his book, *Der Genius des Krieges und der*

---

* Hans Siemens *Der grosse Betrug* in the *Handbuch der Friedensbewegung*.

Deutsche Krieg (*The Genius of War*), and he, like many
others whose noble Christian principles are undoubted,
not only believes that there is honour in war, which is
true, but that there is in it more honour than dishonour,
more blessing than curse.

Speaking, for instance, of the terrible destruction of
works of art and culture, Scheler argues that it is only
the outward manifestation of culture that can be
destroyed, not culture itself by which we look into the
world of art—that cannot be destroyed : and even if the
outward manifestations are destroyed it will drive the
real art or culture deeper down to its source. We are
not to look on the highest works of culture as the
products of peace. Go deeper and you will see that
they have been conceived and born in blood and iron.
This even justifies, Scheler tells us, the destruction of
Rheims Cathedral, " the exulting noise of German
cannon being really kinder and nearer in harmony
with the spirit of its builders than the lamentations
of the civilised world over its ruin."

It is, of course, true that souls and morals are of
more worth to humanity than art. If works of art
are destroyed, the spirit which gave them birth lives
on, and perhaps the next generation may produce
something still more beautiful than that which has
been sacrificed in the clash between two nations. The
great question remains whether along with the body,
the soul of culture is not destroyed.

If Cologne Cathedral were destroyed by an advancing
army, because there was an observatory on its roof,
would Germany believe that this was done in the
name of the soul of Gothic Art ? or if the dome of St.
Peter's were destroyed by cannon should we consider
that there was in that destruction one breath of the
spirit of its mighty creator, Michelangelo ?

War is not professedly waged for the things of the

spirit, but in the name of soulless might or unscrupulous self-intent. Nor is it true that war leads to the ending of wars or that it has increased the spirit of art and culture more than Peace. To say that the spirit of struggle does this would be much nearer the truth. Certainly struggle and unrest are more artistically and culturally productive than peace and quiet.

It is not even true that war increases physical development. There is not much blessing for the body in blood-soaked trenches. Twenty to thirty million were wounded, so that of the seventy-five million, only thirty million escaped untouched. That, even, is not the whole toll. The best were sacrificed and so the whole race has suffered. It is the survival of the unfittest. This is what destroyed the Roman Empire, and it was the same in France after the Napoleonic wars. And we have said nothing of the frightful increase of such diseases as tuberculosis, nor of the war-born mania for morphia and cocaine.

B. The Moral Destruction.

We believe that in spite of our judgment on it, out of war as out of other evils, even out of sin, good does come, as for instance, when war is a means of executing justice.

Justice ! Is not that the word which justifies War, a word of deep moral significance ? Is not the moral gain greater than the evil ? If that were so, whatever might be said on the other side, we should be compelled to bless it.

But, on the contrary, however much war might help us in the world's development, if it injures morality, we must condemn it. Even Scheler allows this, though he positively considers war as a still active factor in the cause of civilisation. War must, he maintains, be justifiable before the bar of the moral conscience and the religious sense of the race. If that is not the case, those would be right, however weak their voice and their protest, who denounce war with no mitigation.

Undoubtedly war does give wonderful opportunities for the display of moral greatness—and this especially in the beginning, when the expectations of the wonderful opportunities of war are still fresh. This is the case in every great decision by which men are very deeply stirred. In the day of peace a man may be weak and easy going : " But war develops strength ; lifts things out of the common, even discovers courage in the coward."* The awful task, in the struggle between life and death, of helping by personal bravery and endurance in a decision affecting the world's history— knowing too that at any moment a man might appear before the Judgment Seat of God—all this brought out tremendous fortitude and strength of will in the last war, and gave men a great moral dignity. Fr. Dreiling O. F. M., tells us that only a few of the men maintained a very high moral standard to the end of the war.

Yes, a few ! Men get accustomed to anything, even to the most terrible experiences. So much so that they lose all power of thought and live from hand to mouth. War may be a short cut, *if it does not last long*, to a moral and religious awakening ; but if it continues for long it is full of danger to religion and morality. Sincerely devout men became indifferent and stupefied and one company of Bavarians simply declined any religious observances till the Battle of the Somme was over.

But this war-induced indifference is not the worst result. The Commandments of God are trodden underfoot far more ruthlessly than in peace time.

---

* Schiller, *Bride of Messina.*

Faith and trust in God may grow in some souls, but most, even of those who feel the want of Religion, break down and become Godless. One of the wounded during the Battle of the Somme in 1916 said, " Before Verdun we prayed. Now in the Somme we curse everything we see." Fr. Dreiling says, " War is in most ways such a complete contradiction to Religion that the Religion soon becomes simply compassion. Men's minds were full of doubt."

All landmarks were destroyed. " How is it," one was constantly asked, " that the very best people are the ones who have suffered the most, whilst the wicked and unprincipled have prospered ? How can the Good, the all-wise God allow such a war ? How could the God of love have made man such that he could bring about such a horror ? Trust in God and Prayer are senseless. Chance and necessity rule everything in war. This madness, this gigantic fraud is the mockery of all we have till now heard of God and Christ ? " This was the common talk during the later years of the war. " It is folly," they said, " to bring God into it at all. If after all these centuries Religion, especially the Religion of Love, does not make such a war impossible, then its influence on mankind is not worth much."

To many, such thoughts came for the first time, to others, what had been in their minds in the abstract now became concrete and definite.

It is impossible to shield those responsible for the war from the bitterness caused by this destruction of Faith. If we would justify God and Christianity to the soldiers and to the *vox populi*, there is only one thing possible, and that is to acknowledge its truth. There may be exaggeration, but Christianity must be most deeply ashamed of having fallen so far below its ideal. God is not responsible. Men made the war, planned it, broke down all restraints quite light-heartedly, and were too avaricious, too revengeful, too greedy, in one word, too conscienceless to end it when they saw its uselessness and its horror.

We see a further dark side of war if we think of the fourth, fifth, sixth, seventh and eighth Commandments —Thou shalt keep God's Laws with regard to Society : Thou shalt not kill, nor hate, nor break the marriage bond, nor commit other impurities.

War is not in itself murder.   Murder means unlawful killing, destroying the adversary without observing the laws of conflict.   The soldier comes in the name of the State, to fulfil the orders of the State in the struggle : this struggle is announced to the opponent by the declaration of war, and from that moment both armies hold themselves justified in killing.   Man does not fight against man, but impersonal group against impersonal group.   Still, we must not forget that in this last war, quite against former traditions, the word *Massen-mord* (the murder of masses) became quite common, and murder was spoken of quite commonly by those who knew most about it, acknowledging that it was no more a question of a justifiable and knightly struggle.   The German Bishops issued a Pastoral in August 1923, in which they say the world " cannot get out of the poisonous atmosphere of the war, cannot contemplate the disarmament of their armies of millions and it wastes more time and money in making more terrible means of destruction and instruments of murder."

Victory is brought about much more by machines than men—machines whose murdering work men cannot even control.

The whole character of war is changed since the advent of the machine gun.   Now men are shot down in hordes by an enemy they cannot see and who cannot see them.   Undoubtedly the individual soldier does often display a wonderfully fine and chivalrous spirit, and the diabolical modern system is in no way his fault.

Clausewitz, the German classic authority on practical warfare, says that " War is an act of violence by which our enemy is compelled to do our will."* Let us ask our men in the first ranks whether, in bare self-defence, knightly bearing was possible or whether the only possibility was just raw, brutal fighting. Modern warfare has kept little of the nobility of war. A practical soldier, Schücking, writes : " Everything must go under in war. Not to be cruel is folly. Prisoners must not be spared for they may be traitors. Humanity is directly opposed to war. Theft, rape, violence of all kind, are the very essence of war."†

Wilhelm II., speaking to men going to the Chinese War in July 1900, says : " When you come before the enemy, he is to be killed. *No quarter given, no prisoners made,* who falls unto your hands falls. As the Huns made a name for themselves a thousand years ago under King Attila, so now you must behave yourselves that never again may a Chinese man dare to look a German in the face."

What greed or ambition does not excuse is justified by the plea of necessity. Certainly ! Necessity knows no law is a better excuse, but even necessity does not excuse the violation of elementary moral obligations for if necessity knows no law, the keeping of any of the Commandments of God can be evaded.

Nor is the plea rational, though we destroy ruthlessly the bodies of our enemies, we may have tender consideration for their souls.

Scheler truly says that our Lord tells us that we are

---

* *Vom Kriege*, 1905, Chap. I.
† *Die Menschheit* 10, *Jahrgang*, Nr. 38.

not to hate our enemies. Solovjeff thinks differently !
If we love our enemy, he ceases to be our enemy, and
war would come to an end. Christ should have said
not Love your enemies, but, Do we have any
enemies.

We can understand this paradox of loving our
enemies if we think of the enemies of God. He loves
them yet punishes them. So it is thinkable that war
might be waged in love, might be a war of salvation ;
but warfare, as we have seen it, is very far from this,
far from saying that " Christians should strive as if
they did not strive."

Again, sins against sexual morality, adultery and
unnatural sins, are frightfully increased in time of war.
It is, after all, not surprising that men who have been
in the hell of the trenches, cut off from all the amenities
and decencies of ordinary life, should, when they
returned from them, break loose for a short time from
all restraint. It was the same immediately before
troops were sent up to the front line. The Chaplain
noticed that the Sunday before many men and officers
who could perfectly well have been at Mass were
absent—amongst them many who had even been
regular communicants. That night the *Maisons tolérées*
of the town were stormed, a soldier observed cynically,
" They are practically starving." It was a sign that
the regiment was going into special danger.

But the licence of individuals is not the worst feature.
The worst is the recognition and approval of the system,
the providing opportunities for vice. According to
modern ideas, brothels for soldiers are as much a
necessity as baths or hospitals. But what does the
Christian conscience say ? What would Christ or John
the Baptist, St. Paul or St. Chrysostom say to those
Princes and Excellencies who had these centres of sin
erected in masses for men who were looking death daily

in the face, on the excuse that the men were thereby better able to fight.

It is the same with every moral law that we compare with war. We cannot reconcile the Seventh Commandment, " Thou shalt not steal," with the sins against property of a long war. While as to the Eighth Commandment, the English Jesuit, Fr. Keating, says in an article, " Of Peace when there is no Peace " (Month February 1922): " One of the strongest arguments against war is that it necessitates a systematic spreading of falsehood in order to circumvent the enemy. The enemy must be painted absolutely black and accused of every imaginable cruelty, as a monster outside the pale of human consideration. If this is not done the hateful work of killing and being killed would be impossible."

Kant rightly says that the days of thanksgiving for Peace should be followed by a day of Penitence, to ask pardon in the name of the State, for the many sins that have been committed and for the attitude towards other nations of overbearing pride which preferred to vindicate its independence by war rather than by a less aggressive attitude.

C. WAR AND MISSIONARY WORK.

Even numerically the Church suffers through war. There are many who are so upset by the moral upheaval and the terrible conditions they have witnessed that they have simply left the Church.

Pius XI., in his Peace Encyclical, *Ubi Arcano*, speaks of the apostacy of Priests caused by the war. But the Mystical Body of Christ must not only be careful not to lose numbers, She must be ever on the alert to win to Herself New Numbers, Her Missionary zeal must be unfailing.

War shows no consideration to Missioners. In German East Africa 26,000 Catechumens were unbaptised, 55,000 native school children left without teachers and relapsed into heathendom. Abbot Norbert of St. Ottilien, writes in January 1918 that 2,260 Mission priests were taken from their stations by force, 1,500 Lay Brothers and 2,000 Mission Sisters re-called.

Mission work has suffered inconceivably by the war. Native Christians are living without the Sacraments, and dying without Priests. The Kingdom of God suffers and is unconsidered whilst new boundaries are being settled.

What must the heathens have thought when they heard how non-combatants, women and children and the aged, were treated as the result of European civilisation. The Indian Tagore writes to the Japanese to warn them against this civilisation, and the testimony of Buddhists and Brahmins at the Religious Congress at Chicago is even more emphatic. They say to us European Christians, " You send your missionaries to preach your faith to us. We do not deny its worth, but after an experience of two hundred years we see that your life is a complete contradiction to what you preach, that you are not led by the spirit of Love, but by the spirit of self-seeking and brute force, which is what rules in all wicked men, so either your Religion is not true and is useless ; or else you are so bad that you do not attempt to do what you could and ought to do. In either case, we are not concerned with you and you must leave us in peace."

Is there any way of deliverance from this shameful and terrible position into which the war has plunged the Christian World? Yes, but only one way. We must give up trying to square the spirit of war with the Spirit of Christ. We must acknowledge that they can no more amalgamate than can fire and water.

Christians may fight when they must, but to love war and to embark upon it without the most absolute necessity is to fall from the spirit of Christ ; it is to put the mystical Christ to death. " Self-murder and madness " is what Clement of Rome calls it in the First Century, and Benedict XV. used the same words of the World War at Christmas 1916, and so with the voices of the best of our leaders and teachers we can answer our heathen accusers. No objection can be made to the real attitude of Christianity to war, but if a Christian country goes to war without absolute necessity, it is practically acting as un-Christian. War is an explosion of un-Christian force for which Christians are not individually responsible, but they are all indirectly responsible in so far as they have not sufficiently developed their own strength and influence. So we must conclude always with an acknowledgment of guilt and a resolve to overcome the madness of war in future.

CHAPTER III

THE METAPHYSICAL AND MORAL PROBLEM

A. THE NECESSITY OF WAR
B. JUST AND UNJUST WAR

    (1) IN THE NATURAL LAW

    (2) IN REVELATION
        (*a*) IN THE OLD TESTAMENT
        (*b*) IN THE NEW TESTAMENT

CHAPTER III

THE METAPHYSICAL AND MORAL PROBLEM

A. THE NECESSITY OF WAR

WAR is an appalling evil. The Prayers of the Church
speak of it in the same breath as pestilence and famine,
though pestilence and famine are not on the same level
as war, because they are nearly always the result of war
and because they are not due to human will. War
is not only an evil as pestilence and famine are ; it is
not only blood shedding, but it is the exaltation of every
physical, mental and moral evil. That war is an evil,
almost everyone, certainly every Christian, must allow,
but the majority considers it a necessary evil, to be
borne as something that cannot be avoided.

Perhaps one of the sharpest divisions between
spiritually and materially minded men is that the
materially minded only know *Facts*—riches and poverty,
content and discontent, progression and retrogression.
For the spiritually minded man, the most ordinary
matters of daily life are *Problems*—they make him think
of the meaning of Facts. For the one, war is merely
an occurrence that comes and goes like pleasure and
suffering. The other ponders over the meaning of
war, its metaphysical origin, its right or wrong, the
possibility or impossibility of its prevention.

War seems always to have been a normal factor in

47

the world's history.   Johann von Bloch* writes that
although, for civilised countries war is not by any means
perpetual, yet taking the world as a whole, from 1496
B.C. till 1861 A.D. there have only been two hundred and
twenty-seven years in which there was no war anywhere
—one year of peace to thirteen of war, so that we may
say that war is almost the world's normal state.

This state of things cannot be quite independent of
the Divine Government.   We are faced by the question
whether God positively wills war as an element in His
ordering of the world.   One of the laws of nature given
by God is the struggle for existence which must lead to
a warlike spirit and it seems that God leads up to war
directly, whether by an unmistakable manifestation of
His Will or by simply leaving men and circumstances to
themselves and using their conduct for the fulfilment of
His Desires.

Thus we ask whether this fact of the constant recurrence of war springs from a direct or an indirect law
of God.

Undeniably struggle is one of the main conditions of
life.   Development and destruction are ever allied in
the world of nature and of men.   Nothing living can
escape this conflict.   The law runs through the vegetable
and animal world up to man.   With man as with the
rest of creation this law of struggle drives him on, but
there is also the lust, even when necessity does not drive
him, to try his strength, to use that power which is his
birthright.   Man is by nature not only a ruler, but also
a conqueror.   The more alive his spiritual and physical
powers are, the more he longs to rise, to increase his
influence, improve the conditions of his life, to step
forward in every way.   All this is quite legitimate and
can take place without any failing in duty or any wrong.

---

* *Der Krieg*, 6 Bände, Bond 1, Einl. xi.

It can be a sign of natural perfection, even of likeness, to the image of God.

Yet even the unreasoning beasts do not blindly destroy one another. They work together for mutual support and fellowship. And with man likewise the law of conflict must be limited and hedged round by the law of mutual fellowship, of consideration for his fellows, for all the animate and even the inanimate creation. Is it even truer to say of man that he is by nature a worker than to say that by the laws of nature he is a fighter. That he is not primarily intended to be a fighter is shown in this, that he is not provided with any natural weapons. He has no horns, or hoof, nor poison in his teeth, nor natural coat of mail. He is primarily equipped to be a worker and is given his *hand*. Nor is it fair that the talents which make man fitted for a life of peaceful labour should be used for war. Is not that against the laws of nature ? Must man, who by nature is a peaceful worker and under certain conditions a fighter and ruler and conqueror, be also by nature a warrior ? Is it right and fair that because of the original sin of fallen human nature, war is to be a necessity ? The result of man's fall is that personal sinfulness, suffering and death have become unavoidable ; but it in no way follows that any *particular* sin or result of sin is unavoidable, and therefore neither the sin of war nor the sinful results of war. Unfortunately it is very necessary to emphasise this truth as strongly as possible for we are always being told that war is a law of nature.

The Romans went even further and maintained that the state of war was the natural state of nations towards each other—that *Pax* was the result of *pacisci*, that Peace was only subjection to the Roman Legions.

Hobbes also taught that war was the natural state and peace only the subjection of special groups bound

D

by an artificial contract. When war breaks out the
natural condition is restored ; when peace comes again
nature for the time is thrust back. We may not hear
these very extreme theories to-day, but we still are told
that history teaches the necessity of war. Bismarck
said in 1891, " War is a law of nature. It is the struggle
for existence in a general form and till men become
angels it will not cease." Here we have a mixture of
truth and falsehood. Because a thing has happened a
million times, it does not become a law of nature.
The conclusion is false. It is quite true that as long as
mine and thine, man and woman, flesh and spirit exist
there will be sin and suffering : human nature being
what it is, it is impossible to eliminate them from the
world. But does that apply to war ?

Supposing there was no war—that war had come to
an end for ever, should we ask : What has happened
to the Divine ordering of the world ? If sin and
suffering were no more we should say mankind is altered ;
but if war could never be again, we should say that a
particular evil resulting from sin had ceased, as slavery,
for instance, has ceased. For centuries the world's
greatest thinkers, with Aristotle at their head, considered
slavery as part of the Divine unchangeable ordering of
the world. Slavery was *man's* work allowed by God,
brought about by man's perverted will and ended by
man's reformed will. In his Pastoral of 1914 Bishop
Casartelli, of Salford, asks why if the nineteenth century
did away with slavery the twentieth should not do
away with war.

Both slavery and war are incompatible with the
solidarity of the nations. As long as the power of the
slave owner and the weakness of the slave lasted, so
long slavery was looked on as part of the Divine ordering
of the world ; and so long as the present system of
armaments and its result the explosion of war is

considered as a necessity for the State, just so long shall we go on hearing that war is part of the Divine economy. God does indeed hold all things in His Hand, and in that sense it is true to say that war is an element in the Divine ordering of the world.   Anything so tremendous as a war must play a large part in the counsels of God.

In war God weighs the nations in His Scales and passes judgment on them.   But He does not drive man against man in strife by a law of nature or by a direct command.

What is for ever necessary so long as man is man, is struggle.   That harmony which came originally from God in each man's own nature and in his relation to his fellows was disturbed by the Fall.   The flesh is no longer subject, without struggle, to the spirit, and this inner conflict is continued in the outer world.   Man must fight for his life and for the necessities of his existence and in this fight man is his neighbour's adversary.

Each individual will is free—one wants this, one that. Freewill leads men, too, to combine in groups and these groups have a common will which differs from the common will of other groups ; and so there must be struggle as long as human nature is unchanged.

BUT STRUGGLE IS NOT WAR.

If these groups had no trained and equipped army behind them, what we mean by war would be impossible. That is to say, if justice could take the place of force, and a trial by law the place of carnage.   This would certainly make an international police force necessary, but then indeed war, *not struggle*, would be driven out of the world.

War in the meantime is a standing example of the perversity of the human ordering of the world when it is allowed by God to work itself out freely.

D—2

B. JUST AND UNJUST WAR

(1) IN THE NATURAL LAW

If war is looked upon as an ordinary means of struggle, recognised by the law of nations and accepted by the present conditions of society, we ask on what moral grounds it is justified and what are its moral limitations? Just as there is a completely unphilosophical attitude to the metaphysics of war, so there is also an amoral attitude, namely an attitude that takes no heed of the moral side, to the problem of war.

On the boundary line between mere facts and problems stands the theory that the right to make war and the right in war comes simply from the fact of war itself. It is said not to be necessary to justify war by the ordinary maxims of morality, for war bears this justification in itself.

Nietzsche says : " You say that a good cause makes war holy ? I tell you, the good war (i.e. the destruction of your enemy) makes everything holy. All those who rejoice in war for its own sake really pay homage to this philosophy."*

The other less unscrupulous theory which was common before the Great War, is that war is the blood and iron cure for weakness and idleness. Hegel says that war teaches us the vanity of worldly things, and makes that into reality which had hitherto been only edifying talk.† Moltke's saying is well known, " Everlasting Peace is only a dream, not even a beautiful dream, and war is an element in God's Government of the world. It develops in man the noblest virtues, courage and self-denial, love of duty

---

* *Also Sprach Zarthustra.*
† *Rechtsphilosphie,* §324, *Werke,* Band VIII.

and self-sacrifice. Without war the world would sink into materialism."*

The Great War has certainly proved the fallacy of this last opinion. Modern machine warfare may still produce much that is spiritual and good, but its terrible brutality and its imperialistic and capitalistic origin make it far more an orgy of materialism than an influence through punishment, making for something higher and better.

As to the moral justification of war : the morality of an action depends on what is primarily effected by it, not by what its indirect object may have been.

We must put the question then : can war, this awful upheaval, with all its destruction and misery, be in itself permissible ? It is clear that its own lawfulness is not the first consideration ; it is only the means to an end. And what is that end? It can only be the preservation or restoration of justice. When war is only resorted to as a last means—when every other influence has been tried and has failed—of restoring justice, then it is allowable by natural law.

Justice is the highest good on earth. No material good, no undisturbed possession of this world's goods, neither health nor life itself, is of such high worth and dignity as the guarding of justice. If no home was destroyed, no life lost in war, but justice went unvindicated, it would be shameful.

The fact that war is a destroyer bringing much suffering in its wake would not be sufficient cause to forbid it. When war is waged in the name of outraged justice, then is its work of upheaval holier than any consideration of property or life apart from justice.

The purely abstract consideration is theoretically unassailable ; but we ask ourselves where, in the con-

---

* In a letter to Bluntchli, 11 Dec., 1880.

crete world of man and nature, war can really be waged in this high and holy way as the servant of justice and as the protector of the moral ordering of the world.

DEFENSIVE WARS

If, without just cause, one State overruns another, lays waste the land, murders the inhabitants : in a word, treads right and justice under foot, then the State that is attacked has undoubted right to defend itself with armies.

Individuals or nations have the right of defence, and in necessity the right to take their enemy's life to save their own. There is even a deeper principle involved : the shielding of the world's moral order from injustice in the name of God and man. Worse than the attack on human life is the attack on God's order which is destroyed by crime. Where the innocent are saved through the death of the guilty aggressor, the Fifth Commandment is not broken. What is right for the individual is right for the State. If all other means have been tried and have failed, armed defence is justified both in self-defence and in defence of God's moral ordering of the world—God does not will that injustice should go unpunished. The sword must be drawn from the scabbard to resist an unjust attack which can only be opposed by a war of defence.

It will be seen, by the conditions given below, how strongly Catholic Moral Theology, which in this case only interprets the law of Nature, insists that a just cause alone can make a defensive war permissible :

(1) The aggression must be unmistakable. The growth of armaments of other nations is not enough. At the same time it is not indispensable that the enemy should fire the first shot. It suffices that the attack be quite certain—this constitutes the necessity, but—

(2) The Defensive must not exceed absolutely necessary defence, for a great war of defence would become unjust if the attacked, when the tide flowed in his favour, attempted more than to make the attacker harmless, since the only ground for allowing war is that the attack of the opponent was unjust.

(3) If justice was on the opposite side—if, for instance the enemy had gone to war to rectify some great injustice done by the State he is attacking—that State, though on the defensive, would have no right to fight. Justice would forbid any action in opposition—the guilty State must submit to punishment from its adversary.

Now let us ask how often has a war of defence been carried on according to the conditions of the Law of Nature ? If these conditions are considered impracticable, does it necessarily follow that they are foolish ? Not at all. They are entirely just. What follows then from the fact that man and nature are incapable of waging a simply defensive war ? It follows that everyone who has the courage to think the matter out will gravely doubt the practical possibility of such a war as a means to justice.

It is, to begin with, almost impossible to decide who is the original aggressor—whether it is the side which declares war, or that which issues the ultimatum or that which has necessitated the ultimatum. Will any nation acknowledge to-day, when the feeling of responsibility for the war is very much stronger than formerly, that it was the unjust attacker ? Sudden invasions, without any diplomatic announcement, do not take place in these days. No one is now the aggressor in the sense that he could not demonstrate that he was in some degree on the defensive.

In the late war, each State defended or pretended to defend some sacred ideal : Serbia defended herself against absorption by Austria ; Russia and Montenegro defended the peoples of their stock ; Austria her " Prestige " in the Balkans ; Germany her fidelity to her " Nibelungen ideal " (*Nibelungentreue*) ; England defended the rights of neutrals ; Japan the Mongolian interest ; France fought to free the annexed provinces from the oppressor ; Italy to release her subjected Italian brethren ; Armenia for the democratic ideal. Belgium alone fought in self-defence. What Turkey fought for is not apparent, but seemingly she was dragged unwillingly into the fray. These attempts to justify the war by proving it to be purely defensive are so far a move in the right direction in that they show, compared to previous occasions, an increased feeling of the moral responsibility which rests on all Governments in declaring war.

Even if it were proved that a war was strictly defensive, how would the check of the so-called measure of authorised protection really work ? What would be practically impossible is the application of punitive justice, the idea being that only one of the fighting parties should bear the punishment resulting from the war and should submit quietly like a boy being punished by his father.

WARS OF AGGRESSION

It is still more difficult to establish the moral conditions which justify a war of aggression than it is to do so for a defensive war. Theoretically this kind of war can also be justified. We have seen that the justification of defensive warfare is based not only on the right of self-defence, but on something deeper still, i.e. the moral order, which cannot be attacked without sinning against law and also against the author of law —Almighty God. An unjust aggressive war not only wrongs the enemy country and its inhabitants, but there are other ways in which one nation fighting against another incurs guilt. Is this guilt to remain unatoned ?

So long as there is no supernational tribunal with international powers of punishment there will be no atonement unless the aggrieved State defends itself and calls the aggressor to account. This happens when the war is carried into the aggressor's country and the aggrieved party takes the law into his own hands, in default of an arbitrator, and gets satisfaction. This, since the time of Augustine, has been the tradition of the Catholic Church with regard to the justification of an aggressive war. St. Thomas Aquinas states this clearly,* as do Francis de Victoria, O.P., and Francis Suarez, S.J. St. Thomas gives three conditions which make a war just : (1) a declaration of war by the highest authority of the State ; (2) a just reason for going to war ; and (3) the right object in view.

LAWFUL AUTHORITY

The first condition is directed against " the right of the fist " which prevailed in the middle ages, by which every little prince or every citizen thought he had the right to make war.

St. Thomas says that private individuals, by whom he means those who have an earthly ruler over them, should seek justice at his hands. And on this is based the justification of war.

It can only be lawful for a State to help itself in this way when there is no power above the State from which it can obtain justice.

An international court, with authority over all States, whose object was to preserve peace would be the lever

----

* II., IIae qu. 40.

of Archimedes, whereby the whole world could be
raised above war and its miserable substitute of justice.
Given the *judicium superioris* of St. Thomas, endowed
with the necessary authority and strength, and war as
a means of national self-defence is at an end. Till we
have this court, he who has the care of any State must
protect and defend it from its internal enemies and
punish them even with the sword. As St. Paul says
(Rom. XIII., 4), " Let not the powers that be bear the
sword in vain, but they are to be helpers of God and
punish evil doers," so also must the rulers defend their
trust from outside aggression.

There is a second point on which the right to make
war stands or falls, and in the opinion of many it has
fallen ! Max Scheler says : " Many consider untenable
the Thomistic conception of a punitive war (*bellum
punitionis*), but Kant rightly disagrees."* And why ?
" Because between States there is not the relationship
of superior to subordinate."†

The Scholastics recognise the objection that a Power
or a State has no jurisdiction over another State.
Cajetan answers that the right of a State to punish its
own subjects is undoubted. But foreigners must also
submit to punishment if they have sinned against a
State because every State must safeguard its own well-
being. If a State had not the right to punish foreign
peoples and princes, it would be incomplete and
imperfect, for tyrants, robbers, murderers, criminals
of all kinds, who as citizens of other States have done
evil, would avoid all punishment and the national order
would be wanting in just the three things which are
most important."‡

Suarez quotes the Old Testament, where God

---

* Zum ewigen Frieden, 6. Präliminarartikel.
† Scheler, *op. cit.*
‡ Cajetan, Summa S. Thomae, Comm. il. II., IIae, qu. 40.

commanded wars for the punishment of guilty nations.*

This comparison of a direct command of God must not be taken literally, for it only refers to the State where, according to God's rule, it is " A perfect community." Such a State must of course have rights necessary for its well-being. Does the right to punish the foreign enemy extend to warding off aggressive attacks, i.e. to a war of defence ? If this is conceded, how is it reconciled with the Scholastic teaching that the enemy deserving punishment must not defend himself, but accept his chastisement as the act of justice ?

This problem of punitive war goes still further. It raises this great question. Can the guilt of the other State be established, and who can establish it ? Sometimes of course there is no doubt ; but is this generally the case ? And yet according to the Scholastics, firstly, undoubted guilt is the only reason for an aggressive war ; and secondly, this guilt must be only on the attacking side.

JUST GROUND AND JUST INTENTION

St. Thomas's second requirement for war to be permissible is the " just cause " (*justa causa*). He knows one only : that the attacked have deserved to be attacked because of some fault (*ut scilicet illi, qui impugnantur, propter aliquam culpam impugnationem mereantur*). St. Thomas quotes St. Augustine, who defines a just war " as the avenging of injustice, when a State or town is to be punished because its inhabitants have been unjust or have neglected rightful restitution."† Francis de Victoria emphatically requires such deeds of injustice as the one and only justification

---

* De Bello, p. 4.   † *Lib. Qualst.*, VI., 10.

of a declaration of war.* On the authority of St. Augustine, St. Thomas and all the Masters, he says: " Aggressive warfare must have as its object the punishment of unjust dealing. Punishment can only be meted when there has been a fault and an injury to the rights of the aggressor." Also he says : " The Prince has no more authority over foreigners than over his own subjects, but he can use the sword equally against both to punish all unjust deeds. By the law of nature it is murder to kill the innocent."

Clearly from these authorities there must be moral guilt to justify war, and they refer us to St. Paul, who tells us that the Ruler is the helper of God, His avenger of the evil doer.

Vanderpol, in his great work, " *La doctrine Scholastique du droit de la Guerre,*" considers that it is a great loss to humanity that the Scholastic teaching on war has been in abeyance since the seventeenth century. Commenting on the Pauline text, he says : " A servant of God : he must only punish when God Himself would punish—an avenger of His Wrath. He may punish only those whose actions would call for the wrath of God—those who have done evil. He must never use his power against those who have not sinned."

All moral and religious people who mourn over the light-hearted way in which war is begun will be grateful to Vanderpol for having drawn attention to the teaching of St. Paul and St. Augustine, but he will ask himself whether, in the face of the practical experience of many centuries, these theories are possible. To begin with : what rulers or States in declaring war consider themselves as the helpers of God, the avengers of His Wrath ? Therefore, where is the guilt or the guiltlessness ?

---

* *De Bello,* I., 3.

Where is the conflict which on the one side is absolutely just and on the other absolutely unjust ? What are the necessary conditions, according to St. Augustine, and the Scholastics ? And what do we mean by punishing a whole nation ? Is the whole nation ever guilty ? And lastly are these just aggressors sure of being only the avengers of the wrath of God, sure that they only right the wrong ? Is their just and holy mission sure to triumph and to preserve the true meaning of an aggressive war ?

These are serious questions to be answered. To the first we may say that it is not necessary for the aggressor to realise that he is in the place of God. Perhaps not for the *results* of his work of punishment ; but certainly subjectively, for the sake of the purity of his own conscience and the single-mindedness of the way in which he will carry out his terrible task. Only the General and the Army inspired with something like the Faith of the Israelites of old could let loose so terrible a thing as war in the spirit of God and not of the devil.

And now : where is the guilt and where the guiltlessness ? Or is this question of the moral guilt of a just war unimportant ? Till the end of the sixteenth century all Catholic Teachers and Theologians held that only the absolutely certain moral guilt of one of the contending parties gave to the other the right to fight. St. Augustine says : " For the wise (the just and the pious) it is the injustice of the opponent's cause which makes a just war."* He says again : " In a just war the other side is fighting on the side of sin " ;† and lastly : " The good, if they are really good, do not fight against the good. Those who fight are either the bad against the bad, or the bad against the good,‡

---

* *De civ. Dei*, XIX., 7.   † *Op. cit.*, XIX., 15.
‡ *Op. cit.*, XXV., 5.

so never good against good, never the defenders of justice against the defenders of justice."

What is to happen if the apportioning of guilt is doubtful ? A clear moral rule comes in. In positive doubt nothing must be done. Suarez declares that the State that declares war must have no manner of doubt, the grounds of its rights must be clearer than the day. Mistakes are inexcusable. To declare war is to pass sentence of death, and to do that with a doubting conscience is mortal sin.*

Vasquez says that to arrive at certainty, both parties must mutually examine their grounds : not to do so is pure barbarism. But who is to subject his cause to his adversary ? Both parties must do so, for no State could be expected to subject itself to its adversary without reciprocity. In these circumstances, where would the proposed war be ? Nowhere, for each side would see that each had right on his side and a just war is only conceivable as punishment for injustice : and then each side would acknowledge its faults. (O that the world could think and act with the logic of the Scholastics in their Cloister. The world must ! But of that later.)

Clearly such a doctrine, strong but not bitter, yet so opposed to military passion and the so-called interests of the State, would be difficult to enforce. The conduct of States and rulers is so different : but would it be impossible to call them before a moral court ? Should they be allowed to fight if they acknowledged that there was sufficient right on the enemies' side to make the justice of their cause doubtful ?

Suarez is the first who says Yes—that if, after careful examination of the cause of dispute, the prince or ruler considers there is more to be said on his side than on the

---

* *Schol. Com. in* II., I Iae., qu. 40, art. I., dub. 5.

other, then he is justified in going to war. Suarez applies for the first time the principles of distributive justice to war. With St. Augustine and St. Thomas these principles are applied only to an act of vindictive justice. Suarez teaches that a ruler may go to war knowing that a great deal of right is on the opposite side, but considering that, on the whole, more right is on his side ! Here we have the first loosening of the old, strict war morality. The terrors of war are to be let loose because the balance is ever so slightly on the aggressor's side ! though even Suarez recommends an umpire. His point of view is most repulsive, for he holds strongly to the punitive character of the aggressor. " The proofs in criminal matters must be sufficient, but if the crime cannot be proved guilt must be presumed." *

What becomes of justice when an individual or a nation is sentenced to death on the grounds of probable guilt ?

A lively protest was raised against this weakening of the teaching of St. Augustine and the Thomists. Vasquez, in particular, opposed his brother in the Society : " I could never accept such teaching, on the contrary I have always held its dubiousness and believe that it may do great harm to Christianity. That might is right is simply a return to barbarism."†

Molina went further. ‡According to him a *material* injustice on the part of those to be attacked justifies a war of aggression. Thus the high character of war as a means of punishment for grave *moral* guilt ceases. It is true of course that in the case of mere national injustice which Molina had in mind, the unjust possession of something belonging to the other State might be a very

---

* *De Bello*, 7.
† *Com. in Summa St. Thomae, Disp.*, 64, Cap. 3.
‡ *De Justitia et jure*, Paris, 1602, *Tom.* 1, Tract II.

important consideration for that State.   But this unjust
possession either can be proved or cannot be proved.   If
it is proved and the State refused to give up what had
been unjustly acquired, then it is morally guilty, and
by all the rules of morality may be attacked.   If it
cannot be proved, then there is not even a material
injustice, and war is ruled out.   The harm of the war
theory lies just in this carelessness in getting direct
proof of real injustice.   A wrong, an injustice, without
moral guilt is a most doubtful thing, and the old school
is surely right in insisting on proof of this moral guilt
before plunging into the horrors of war.   After the
strict principles of the old School had been tampered
with, excuses for war were made more and more easily.
Not all the sixteenth and seventeenth century Theologians, however, departed from the more perfect teaching
of St. Augustine and St. Thomas.   Sylvius in particular
(1648) remained true to their principles and says :
" When it is a question of imperilling the lives of a
mass of men, the safest way must always be chosen.
If it is a question of possession, he who is in possession is
not bound to give it up, but he must discuss the question
with his adversary, he must receive his ambassadors and
listen to their propositions."   The new School, however,
has been active and busy in its teaching.   War has
been looked upon as a function of commutative
justice.

Vanderpol, on the other side, shows how easy it is on
such grounds to justify a war undertaken for no just
cause, i.e. to keep the so-called balance of power, or to
prevent the extension of a neighbouring state.   This is
all the more important as we find in modern authors no
word as to the moral guilt which ought to be punished
by war.   Things had gone so far that in the nineteenth
century Gousset wrote that " war was justified if it
were ' necessary ' for a nation either to defend it against

invasion or to break down any opposition to the exercise of its rights."* We ask *what* rights.

How does St. Alfonsus Liguori stand to all these questions? He belongs to the new School and adopts its views—specially those of Busenbaum—but he sympathises with those who consider a declaration of war such a serious matter that it can only be justified if there is no possible doubt as to the justice of the cause. He says " War brings such evils with it— such harm to Religion and to the innocent that in practice it is hardly ever justifiable."†

Considering the terrors of modern warfare and their results, and considering also that the Catholic Church *as such* has no defined teaching about war, it is surely permissible to take such a line as to the justifiableness of war as will restrict it as much as possible. This book holds completely to the teaching of St. Augustine and St. Thomas. The deduction we draw from their teaching, that a war of aggression is only allowable when the adversary's guilt is absolutely certain, is that a *just* war of aggression is hardly possible.

The " *justa causa* " must contain two features : moral guilt and certain knowledge of this guilt. A merely judicial or material, i.e., an unconscious guilt, is not enough. It is not an evil deed. Those who commit it are not evil-doers. To declare war on such is forbidden by the laws of nature. Certainly material wrongdoing is to be eliminated from the world, but war is not the means. If we are told that this sets up an unjust state of things, we can truly answer that war does so much more disastrously. Firstly, to go to war on account of a material injustice is immoral and only makes it worse ; secondly it is quite uncertain if the

---

* Gousset, *Theol. mor.*, 1845.
† *Lib.*, III., Tract IV., Nh. 404.

E

injustice will be rectified, and, as a means to the removal of material injustice, war is a failure.

But, before it can be healed, moral guilt requires a cure equal to its enormity. It would be a crime to plunge recklessly into war, even if the fault is proved, without any doubt, to be on the other side. The punishment must be, so far as is possible in earthly justice, in proportion to the moral guilt. For instance, a ruler or ambassador is murdered. This is a great crime committed against some State for political reasons. Should the answer of the injured State be an immediate declaration of war, or even only a short and impossible ultimatum? What are the results? Because one criminal, or group of criminals, commits a crime, millions of innocent people are to be punished in the most terrible ways? Would the real murderers be the sufferers? Supposing even that the injured side wins, is justice appeased when millions of innocent men are slaughtered, others are crippled and maimed for life, women and children are widowed and orphaned, immeasurable property is destroyed? In fact it seems simply the denial of human instincts of right, even though there were no shadow of doubt as to the moral guilt of the conquered State. Instead of a just war would not the following method be better? The State responsible for the political murder should be required to punish the murderer. If this was done adequately there would be no question of war. If not, there should be a referendum of the inhabitants and in modern times the people can practically compel the Government to act as they wish. In this case it would be to insist on the punishment of the murderer and giving such satisfaction as was possible. Only when the majority refused satisfaction, i.e., sided with the murderer, would the question of war be raised as the punishment of moral guilt : and in these circumstances when the country was being dragged into war, the inhabitants would be justified in refusing military service.

But justice also lays a heavy responsibility on the other side before it dares to resort to war. As the meaning of war really is atonement, it must not be entered into unless this object is moderately certain of attainment. Hence Cajetan and Victoria maintain that no war must be begun unless the attacking party is morally sure of victory.

The following point deserves particular notice. Victoria teaches that a town or province has the right of reconquest, and yet, nevertheless, war is forbidden because of its disastrous results. As we have seen, war must only be undertaken in the common interest. For example, if a town can only be retaken at the price of enormous evils, by injuring many other towns, by the murder of countless men, when it would cause enmities amongst Princes, would probably result in further wars, and if it would harm the Church, then the Prince must undoubtedly withdraw from the war, even if its results would include the conversion of the heathen.

For example, suppose the King of France had rights on the Province of Milan, but that war would bring great suffering and distress both to France and to Milan, the King would not be allowed to go to war, as war could only be permitted if it were to benefit both France and Milan. If, on the contrary, it was to injure them it would not be a just war. " A war is not just, if it is evident that it will do the State more harm than good, even if there is ' just cause.' The State has only the right to declare war for self-protection, and the defence of itself and its property. If a war must result in its being weakened then the war is unjust, no matter by what King or State it is declared."

E—2

The leading thought of his book, the necessity of Unity and mutual consideration in the Mystical Body of Christ, is dealt with by Victoria as follows : " A Christian Province is part of a State, a State part of the whole world : so if a war benefits one Province or one State, but injures the whole world or Christendom, I consider such a war unjust."

Thus the School of St. Augustine and St. Thomas limits the right of a State to declare war even when the guilt of the opponent is clear.   The common conception of national honour does not consider the results of war—commonsense and morality, which differ in many respects from this conception, do consider these results and declare this game of hazard, which is war, immoral, and therefore forbidden even when national honour has been insulted and the enemy refuses satisfaction ! Divine and human interests are more important than the interest of the individual State.

Here we have the whole difference between the mediaeval and the modern outlook.   Before the western communities were individualised and rent in pieces, the community interests were in the foreground.   National egoism which thinks only of itself, was condemned even where the ideal involved heavy sacrifice.   After the individual—and also the individual State—became emancipated from the higher obligation to the community, national individual interest became the chief thing and the supernatural interest of the community at large, a side issue.   This does not mean that hitherto there has been no unprincipled self-seeking and trickery in national life, and in the conduct of war, but that there was no moral theory which justified it.   The new individual-istic morality as opposed to the old morality of solidarity is just the *proton Pseudos* of false, modern culture.

The second *justa causa* is the undeniable assurance of moral guilt.   And here let us remember that apart from the actual point at issue, there is the psychological fact to bear in mind that very often the fault exists only in the imagination of the accuser and proceeds from his arrogance, whether it is the individual or the State.

We can see the mote in the eye of another and not the beam in our own. This weighty fact is just as worthy of consideration with regard to the justice of a war as are external circumstances. The catholic Professor of moral theology, John Baptist von Hirscher, lays much stress on this. " The first question," he writes, in his chapter on war, " is, has there been a real unjust insult ? Pride, greed, over-bearingness, love of power, are often hurt, but there need be no injury to justice in the offence but on the contrary, opposition to oppression and greed of possession, unjust annexation, etc. Powerful nations, too, are often condescending and overbearing to their neighbours and intend to insult them if they offer any opposition. No one is free from guilt and all should remember the saying : Do to others as you would they should do to you. If there is real injury, it is for the injured party to complain in a fair and manly, but not offended, manner. If this is not done then the cause must be made public and pleaded before a Court of Nations. Possibly the result of this appeal will be that the wrong will be righted. If not, then the time of necessity and self-help has come. The first step is reprisals—the last step, war."

As regards the " just cause." The old moralists forbid war if it can be found that the unjustly accused side had given great provocation. If the Thomists do not acknowledge a war to be just on both sides, it does not follow that they do not acknowledge a cause of strife that is justifiable on both sides, all they ask is that no doubtful case should lead to war. Right and wrong can be so shared by both sides that humanly speaking it is impossible to apportion the blame.

" Right," Lammasch says, " is not always on one side and falsehood and mere bluff on the other. Often it is only a question of forcing the original cause of war far enough back. War may be justifiable from the immediate point of view and unjustifiable if we look further back for the cause. Unless we can unravel the original causes we cannot say whose is the original guilt. State A has wronged State B centuries ago. The bitterness and hate have simmered for ages, and finally State B does something which State A considers a just cause of war."*

It may well be said that the State that makes war, never has believed in its own wrong and the right of its adversary. It has always considered that there were justifiable grounds for attack or self-defence. For instance, Mohammedans were convinced of the justice of their Religious wars—Christians equally convinced of their injustice. In modern times we remember the Royal Proclamations on both sides. King William, in 1866, declares : " Austria will not forget that her Princes once ruled Germany and she will therefore only see in young Prussia an enemy rival instead of an ally, and consider that she must always oppose Prussia because what benefits her harms Austria. An old, unholy jealousy burns fiercely again. Prussia is to be weakened, and dishonoured. Faith is not kept with her. Wherever we in Germany look, we are surrounded by enemies and their war-cry is the humiliation of Prussia. To the last minute I have sought and left open the path to a friendly solution, but Austria does not will it."

The Emperor Franz-Josef, on the same day, issued the following proclamation : " The latest events show unmistakably that Prussia puts Might in the place of

---

* *Volkermond oder Volkerbund*, Haag, 1920.

Right and therefore this unholy war of German against German is inevitable. I call him who is responsible for it before the Judgment Seat of God to answer for all the misery he is bringing on nations and individuals."

And on which side was the *justa causa?* If war broke out now between France and Germany both would be convinced that they had right on their side. Therefore we may be sure that only history—namely a later generation—can possibly judge fairly as to who is responsible for a war. In the excitement of political conflict, it would be impossible so to prove the moral guilt of the opponent that no doubt would remain, and yet an absolute certainty is necessary for the justification of war.

St. Thomas's third condition for a just war is *a right intention (intentio recta)*. His definition is : " The intention to further Good and avoid Evil. For, says St. Augustine, in *De verbis Domini*, ' With the true servants of God even wars make for Peace, as they are not undertaken for greed and cruelty but for the sake of Peace, that the wicked may be restrained and the good protected. Therefore it may be that a war is declared by lawful authority and for a ' just cause ' and may yet not be justifiable because the intention of those undertaking it is wrong. For what Augustine rightly blames in war, is the desire to harm, the cruelty of revenge, a vindictive spirit, the rage of self-defence, the lust of power and such like.' "*

It is truly difficult to justify war. For it is to be not only just but quite free from evil intent and ugly passions. Has there ever been a war without the " wish to harm " (*nocendi cupiditas*) or without " the lust of power " (*libido dominandi*), and " such like " ?

---

* II., IIae, 40, 1.

THE RIGHT WAY

Suarez and Bellarmine add a fourth condition to the three of St. Thomas, namely : *debitus modus*—the right way of conducting war.

Victor Cathrein, S.J., defines it in the following terms : " The conduct of the war must be confined within the limits of justice and love."* This condition deserves special notice when it is applied to modern warfare.

War comes up every hour against " the limits of love and justice," and it would indeed be difficult to remember them always. But one limitation must surely always be held sacred : the difference between combatants and non-combatants, between armed and unarmed. It is dishonourable to bear arms against those who cannot defend themselves—against old people, women and children, indeed against civilians at all. In fact it is against military law, except in absolutely unavoidable circumstances, i.e., the siege of a town when civilians have to share the soldiers' fate. Their injury is then, even in just war, quite unavoidable ; but if done intentionally it becomes a crime crying to Heaven for vengeance.

The whole of Catholic Moral Theology forbids in the strongest terms the injury or killing of unarmed *persons*, with direct intention, and condones it only *per accidens*, namely, when unavoidable. This follows from the old view of war as the punishment of guilt— those carrying arms were considered the guilty—the civil population innocent. This distinction, of course, takes for granted that the soldiers have joined the army to go to the help of their Ruler of their free will,

---

* *Moralphilosophie*, II., S., 744., Freiburg, 1911.

and do not belong to a conscript army, the members of which are really in the position of innocent citizens. The old authorities call those fighting for the unjust cause " guilty," but the non-combatants " innocent " ; and they lay down that it is never justifiable to kill the innocent by direct intention—*per accidens* is the only justification. Francis de Victoria says " We must be careful that war does not bring with it greater evils than it is to cure. If a decisive victory depends on the destruction of a fortress or garrison containing a number of innocent, defenceless people, it is not permissible to sacrifice them in order that a lesser number of the guilty should be punished. Let the tares grow with the wheat—lest in pulling up the tares the wheat is pulled up too."

To-day the idea of punishing moral guilt is forgotten, but the distinction between innocent and guilty remains : and the newest idea is that even this should be done away with. It is certain that modern military technique no longer takes the distinction into consideration. Poison Gas Warfare is specially directed against the civil population, which is a sufficient proof of its injustice and its criminal murderous character.

SUMMARY

If we consider the conditions which justify a war from the standard of Catholic morality we find that war is almost an impossibility. Defence or restoration of justice are the only justifications for war. As faith in attaining these ends by means of war slowly dis-

appears one also finds that Catholic authors are restrict-
ing more and more the occasion when war may be
considered permissible.

Hirscher has already taught " that before the bar
of justice and morality only a defensive war that protects
inalienable possessions can be justified and that, only
after every other means has been tried and has failed.
An offensive war between nations is just what robbery,
murder and violence are between individuals, but robbery,
murder, and violence on what a scale ! A war for any
subordinate interest, however undeniable the claim
may be, is always against the spirit of Christianity.
If it concerns possessions which a nation will miss why
not let it be ? ' Rather suffer wrong gladly ' applies
to nations as much as to individuals, and wrong suffered
for God's sake and for the sake of peace will never
bring dishonour."*

The exalted Christian ideal that for nations to suffer
injustice brings with it no shame is so completely opposed
to the standard of modern statecraft, that it is not
surprising that in no other book on Moral Theology do
we find such teaching. We have to look for the Christian ideal in the teaching of men like Tagore.
Certainly Eberle does not acknowledge an aggresive
war as just. He maintains that the only moral justification of war is necessity—a war, defensive and really
preventive.† The modern writer, Schulemann, in
1923 says : " On the whole only defensive wars can
be just."‡

Max zu Sachsen explains that " The state should only
be allowed to make war when the alternative is to be
literally overrun, so that it is compelled to defend itself

---

* *Die christliche Moral*, III., 5, 714, Tübingen, 1838.
† *Krieg und Frieden im Urteil chr. Moral*, S.8.
‡ *Kern aller Philosophie*, S.138.

to avoid destruction."* Even if others take a laxer view of an offensive war, all Catholic moralists condemn a war undertaken for any reason short of gross injustice. According to unanimous Catholic teaching, all are unjust when undertaken for national or dynastic interests, from covetousness or lust of conquest (Imperialism or lust of annexation), wars manoeuvred by Cabinets or religious wars, in fact the overwhelming majority of all past wars. Their authors are, perhaps, to be excused, as they acted in the spirit of their surroundings, but they in no way deserve to be honoured by national memorials or extolled in patriotic verse. The verdict of the Christian conscience is quite different. With St. Augustine it calls an unjust war, even of its own country, " a gigantic robbery."

Here we come across the old teaching of St. Augustine and the Thomists, supported by Suarez and Bellarmim, with their four conditions of a just war. It may seem strangely out of place in the world of to-day, fit only for the Cloister from which it came—so much the worse for the world ! During the last centuries the world's conscience has been so darkened and confused by nationalism and militarism that it can no longer grasp any national moral idea. Woe to morality if it capitulate. Morality must not adapt itself to men, but men to morality, even if the accepted point of view has to be broken down. *Fiat justitia pereat mundus*, the world will say scornfully, but no, *Fiat justitia floreat mundus*, we must and we will say. European civilisation has collapsed not because of the war-morality of the middle ages, but because of the war-immorality of the new age. If there is to be any improvement the moral anarchy must be overcome which has arisen between different

---

* Max zu Sachsen *Ratschläge und Mahnungen zum Volks- und Menscheitswohl.*

States, from the idea of the absoluteness of the State. The *lex aeterna*, which is above all States and which makes for justice, must once more be the foundation of the State. By the necessary limitation of their rights the nations will not be weakened but, on the contrary, strengthened. The world, civilization, society, the Church, are all crying out that war may be overcome. A simply sentimental sense of need is not enough and cannot satisfy any thinking man. The ending of war, or at least the possibility of its being reduced almost to nothing, must be founded on a clear, thought-out, moral system. We believe that the Augustinian-Thomist theory can render this service to the world and to the Church. Just because it makes war's *raison d'être* so difficult, it is the most practical and useful theory that can be thought out and fits in with the new moral consciousness which has been born of the agony of the world war. The modern conscience asks imperatively for that *judicium superioris*, that tribunal of justice above all State courts and rights of nations, the failure of which alone, according to St. Thomas, justifies war. The modern conscience is occupying itself in an unprecedented manner with the moral guilt of war. That war is the affair only of princes and statesmen is no longer believed. Never has war been so generally considered a crime. Men are asking that the moral guilt should be declared and the guilty sharply punished. Such an attitude was unknown ten years ago, and it is precisely the Augustinian conception of the responsibility of the State. If this guilt can never be established without doubt then so much the better, for there is no cause for war and it must not be declared. The best teaching is that which makes it most difficult to find a ground for war, which always takes the arms out of the hands of one party—and on the Augustinian and Thomist principles in no war are both parties in the right—and gives the citizens a handle to justify them in declining to fight. This was the teaching till the seventeenth century of the Catholic Schools ! On one side, a war is always unjust. Augustine says of war that it is a struggle for sin. Cajetan declares that an unjust war is in itself a mortal sin.*

" No authority," says Francis de Victoria, " can command the death of the innocent, and in an unjust war the enemies are innocent, therefore it is not permissible to kill them. The ruler who declares such a war is guilty, and not those only who do evil but those also who agree to it, are worthy of death (Rom. I., 32). Even if the ruler gives the order, a soldier must not put innocent citizens to death and it follows that if a soldier is convinced of the injustice of a war he must not take part in it, for anything that is against a man's conscience is sin."† As to the " just cause " the ordinary soldier is probably not able to judge but he can do so as to the " intention, the *intentio recta*—and as to the way the war is conducted, for the *intentio recta* according to St. Thomas consists in seeking good and avoiding evil, and the ordinary citizen can certainly form an opinion on this, especially as to the right way—the *debitus modus*. If this *modus* transgresses the demands of morality, the war, according to St. Thomas, is unjust and the soldiers must not take part in it. Victoria and others consider that it is not the *duty* of the private soldier to enquire into the justice of a war, but that he has the *right* to do so and Victoria says : " The injustice may be so flagrant that ignorance can be no excuse, otherwise the unbelievers who followed their leaders into wars against Christians and murdered them would be blameless, or the Roman soldiers who crucified

---

* Cajetan *Summula V., Bellum.*
† *De jure belli*, II., 2.

Christ at the command of Pilate."* This question of the right of freedom of conscience in taking part in war is a fiercely contended point to-day, and the question of refusing military service comes up. There may be much that is ignoble, unheroic and materialistic, connected with it ; obedience to rightful authority in everything not opposed to the Christian conscience and that is not sinful, is of course a plain duty, but refusing to serve can be justified on the highest Christian principles, specially when the sinfulness of modern warfare is considered. Further, it is extremely dangerous when this modern movement against war threatens to be, like the devils who were driven out by Beelzebub, the prince of the devils, the reckless revolutionising of the masses against lawful authority, and the unchecked rule of individualism. But it is therefore all the more necessary that the protest against the boundless arbitrariness and barbarity of modern war should find an echo where the greatest spiritual and moral power is still enthroned : on the rock of Peter. It must be confessed that the protest against the exaggerated power of the State and military ruthlessness, and the right, in certain cases, to deny obedience to the State, can be confirmed by appealing to Tradition, Holy Writ and to the noblest authorities of the Church teaching and the Church taught.

That classical teaching of peace and justice, which has been formulated by the greatest teachers of the Church, Augustine and Thomas Aquinas, must stand against modern anarchical Pacifism for the thought on which it is grounded was unquestioned till the seventeenth century and belongs to the future as much as to the past.

The following ten points contain the principles which constitute a just war according to St. Augustine, the Thomists, and Francis de Victoria :

---

* *De jure belli*, I., II.

1.—Gross injustice on the part of one, and only one, of the contending parties.

2.—Gross *formal* moral guilt on one side—material wrong is not sufficient.

3.—Undoubted knowledge of this guilt.

4.—That war should only be declared when every means to prevent it have failed.

5.—Guilt and punishment must be proportionate. Punishment exceeding the measure of guilt is unjust and not to be allowed.

6.—Moral certainty that the side of justice will win.

7.—Right intention to further what is good by the war and to shun what is evil.

8.—War must be rightly conducted : restrained within the limits of justice and love.

9.—Avoidance of unnecessary upheaval of countries not immediately concerned and of the Christian community.

10.—Declaration of war by lawful authorised authority exercised in the name of God.

Failing these conditions war is unjust. Whether they have been fulfilled, in the past or in the present, or are likely to be fulfilled in the future, the reader must decide.

If they are impossible of realisation in the present political condition, perhaps in the future a League of Nations may make them possible. If this could be, an army of police would be necessary for the punishment of any rebellious member of the League. We should then have the assurance that justice, established by the tribunal of rights, would stand fast against injustice, that order would be maintained against disorder. The world would be protected, those who infringed the rights of others would be punished because this League would be powerful and would have military support behind it, to be used in the most harmless manner possible.

This would all be the result of the Augustinian and Thomist teaching on guilt and punishment. The work of proving guilt ought not to be the task of one state—specially the State involved, since no one can judge for himself, but rather of a court of justice which is superior to the disputing parties, and the work of carrying out punishment would belong more to the Police than to the military. The Augustinian-Thomist principles stand also emphatically for the everlasting unchangeable demands of natural right and for the right of nations as taught by the most modern school of Pacifists. The codified law of nations no longer troubles about the moral justification of a war : that would be going back to the dark ages. The teaching which has been here set forth is the synthesis of the old and the new. Our motto must be, " Backward and forward to St. Augustine and to St. Thomas Aquinas."

(2) IN REVELATION.

(a) IN THE OLD TESTAMENT.

The examination of natural law with regard to war as a whole reveals much that is unnatural and wrong. The unending and destructive struggle of man and man shows such degeneration as can only be accounted for by the Christian doctrine of the fall : but even so war is not a necessity. It always has depended on man's freewill and always will. It is only necessary when, how and for so long as man wills it. Man is, therefore, responsible for war. Only as the last resource of justice and under quite exceptional circumstances may the State employ it as the Hand of God to avenge His wrath against evildoers.

Revelation tells us that in certain circumstances and for certain purposes God has Himself put this instrument into the hands of man. The Old Testament speaks of wars undertaken by the Chosen People in the Name of God and carried on at His command. Some critics do not take these passages literally. Max von Sachsen says : " This is the Old Testament language which refers everything that happens to the ordering of God." Origen, who was absolutely opposed to war, considered the Old Testament wars as allegorical and typical—as shadows and pictures of spiritual and moral combats against sin and the powers of darkness, foreshadowing the great fight of Christ and His people against these powers. According to him not even in the Old Testament is there a God of war : " Unless the terrible stories of wars in the Old Testament are to be considered allegorical, the Disciples of the Lord Jesus who came to teach peace, would never have allowed them to be read in Church." On the same grounds Bishop Ulfilas left the war books out of his translation of the Bible, but even if we acknowledge them, and accept as true that God ordered war, it only means that He did so in very exceptional circumstances. It certainly follows that not every war is necessarily immoral and to be condemned, as God cannot approve of anything immoral even to gain the most holy ends. It is possible that something in itself wrong may be ordered by God for some special object, and in that way become right. For instance, a child killed by its father. If God commands such an act, as He did in the case of Abraham and Isaac, simply because it is God's Will, it becomes right and moral. It may be so with the wars of the Old Testament that they were not against the moral law simply because they were undertaken in obedience to the command of God and in exceptional circumstances, but even if these wars were not overruling

F

of God's ordinary laws scriptural justification of war cannot be stretched further than to cover these concrete cases. It is not fair, on account of the biblical wars, to justify war for all time as people are so fond of doing. There is also development in Revelation—religious, moral and cultural progress. Nothing is more untrue than to think that Revelation teaches that the world and mankind are never to develop and that everything is the same for all eternity. The Kingdom of Heaven is like the seed hidden in the ground, but which is ever growing till it becomes the great tree and if mankind as a whole, after the fall, is ever developing from such lowly beginnings to a higher culture, so also is this the law of the Kingdom of God. He chose one nation for the realisation of His plan for the government of the world. It was to carry out His ideal, to keep monotheism pure and gradually to permeate the whole human race with the moral principles of the decalogue. For this high object war, in those early days, was necessary as the means whereby to overcome the surrounding nations, sunk in idolatry and wickedness. The object of these wars was to bring these nations into the Theocracy and under the Blessing of the True God—also under the discipline of His yoke, and if the people of Israel wielded the chastening rod of war—they most certainly felt it themselves. The Israelites and the nations surrounding them were to be brought through a hard schooling, through the law of fear and of atoning justice, to a higher dispensation, to a kingdom of peace and love, to the promised reign of Christ the Messiah. Also under the Old Covenant, war had a special ethos. It was the School of God suited to the actual state of human development—the hardships of war braced up a very sensuous nation to physical and moral endurance. It was therefore the Judgment of God, a punishment for sin and also an acknowledgment of the True God because the ever recurring victories of the Chosen People over all their enemies were proof of the divine calling and protection. So it is that the stories and lessons of the Old Testament about the people of God are unique. These wars have a special and sometimes a wonderful character. It can even be said that in them the human leadership was a side issue, a disguise for the immediate acts of God. As we read in the word of God, in Chronicles XXV., 8, " If you think that the strength of war is in the armies, God will let you be overcome by your enemies for it is the Lord's to help and to destroy." To refer, then, to the Old Testament wars as a justification for later ones devoid as these are of any religious object, is quite unfair, and it is equally unfair to drag out Old Testament texts to justify the modern war spirit which completely ignores the Christian revelation and development of the New Testament. If the commands of God for justice and a high standard in war really prove anything, the defenders of this thesis can be answered by their own argument : so be it— God's command justifies war. Show me, then, a command of God which justifies war *as it is to-day*, and I will believe in its righteousness. If you cannot do this, then I must decline to believe, because such a terrible upsetting of all order as modern war brings with it can only be justified by a direct command of God.

This is plainly only an argument *ad hominem* for people who can twist the justification of modern warfare out of the divine commands of the Old Testament.

Would that we could call forth the noble *ethos* and aim which lay beneath the Old Testament wars ! That inspired patriotism was truly of divine origin, the war songs were religious songs, for the Israelite the death of the enemies of Jehovah was a sacrificial act. Would any one dare to compare what Benedict XV. calls the " suicide " of a modern European war, caused as it is by capitalism, imperialism, and militarism run wild, with the conflicts of the Jewish Theocracy?

Lastly the Old Testament shows something nobler than the theocratic war inspiration. The theocratic theories of peace are far more characteristic—first in their infancy but gradually developing. The most perfect periods of Old Testament conceptions of God were the very earliest and the prophetic, those namely which acknowledged the universal being of God.

These were equally the times of peace and peace theories. God's thoughts were of peace and reconciliation for all nations and peoples. It was during the less perfect times of religious faith and thought that God, on account of the hardheartedness of men, condescended to be the ally of one nation only. The Prophets who were the purest interpreters of the Old Testament spirit were above this standpoint. In the light of their teaching the Old Covenant does not appear as supporting war but as overcoming it.

(b) IN THE NEW TESTAMENT.

When we open the New Testament we are in another world. Coming straight from the Old Testament, and from the warlike spirit of the historical and poetical books, the complete absence of such a spirit strikes us all the more sharply. We hear nothing of war's heroism, the national point of view has disappeared, and instead we leave behind us all this earthly glitter. It seems sometimes as if to our Lord the State was a *quantité négligeable*, which, of course, had its rights, which must be respected and whose dues must be paid, but which was not to be weighed in the balance with the Kingdom of God. With what self-assurance our Lord puts Himself above the national customs, how lovingly He welcomes foreigners, foreigners who were repugnant politically and religiously to the Jew. The relation of the Gospel to the State and to armies can only be understood if we take into consideration these hidden matters. In the beginning of the late war a great attempt was made to justify war from the Gospels. In truth our Lord gave no opinion on war either for or against it. He stands above it. Tax collector or captain, priest or pharisee, Jew, Samaritan or Roman, man or woman, matters not. He sees only men, their souls and spirits. The profession of a soldier may be good or bad, like anything else, and it is the same with tax gathering, interpreting the law, marriage feasts or carrying the dead to their graves, even with prayer and Sabbath keeping. If military service, with all it involves, serves to preserve order and righteousness, then our Lord gives it His Blessing. When it leads to outrageous pride, to bullying instead of serving, to oppressing instead of bringing freedom, to devastating instead of protecting, when order and justice are trodden under foot, men and nations hounded one against another, when the life and health of nations are destroyed in the insatiable lust for power and blood, when incredible harm is done to the Kingdom of God, its freedom, its temples, when its souls are trampled down and soiled, then the loving eyes of Christ are turned away and from His sacred lips rings out the terrible sentence " Get thee hence, Satan." It is absurd to compare the horrors of a great war with the military service of the Captain of Capharnaum, and to argue from our Lord's goodness to him that the infamy of the world war would have His Blessing. It is blasphemous to try and reconcile the Spirit of Christ with the swamp of sin such a war is from its beginning to its end. If we want to keep in Christ's or St. Paul's opinion we must not think of the humble soldier of Capharnaum, or of that other who stood by the Cross, startled and amazed by that great sacrifice ; or of Cornelius, the Centurion ; but of those politicians and military leaders, the industrial speculators, and the speculators on the Stock Exchange who play with men's bodies as if they were dice. There is a mighty difference between war *and* war, and as we have seen it is almost impossible, without God's special help, for any war to be so conducted that the requirements of justice and morality are satisfied. It must be caused by very great moral guilt, its object must be the furthering of good and avoiding of evil, and it must be so conducted that the limitations of justice and love are never infringed. A war on such a high plane would be holy. We should bow before it in reverence and Christ Himself with the Gospels in His Hand, would bless it. But put war as it is to-day with its lust of the eye, lust of the flesh, and pride of life before the eyes and heart of Christ ! Would He not turn away weeping, with the words : " The world, oh Christendom, oh mystical Body of which I am the Head, would that thou hadst known the things that belong to thy Peace ? But they are hidden from thine eyes." Each case, each individual soldier, each war, Christ judges as to its justice, and certainly His sentence is not less severe than that of the theologians of the middle ages. It is impossible to say that Christ acknowledged war as the recognised means of arranging international disputes, nor can we allow that the Christian conscience should be reconciled to war because of its periodical recurrence. When our Lord speaks of war and rumours of war, referring either to the destruction of Jerusalem or to the end of the world, He does not prophesy that war is to be a regular occurrence in the Christian era. There is no justification for such an idea. Our Lord tells us that wars are accompanied with terror and fear. In a like manner the Gospel also reckons with the historical fact of sin.   We know that we shall sin again and again, yet we are bound to avoid sin, for ourselves individually and also to influence others to avoid it.   Just such a duty has the Christian about war.   It is the result of sin, but also the cause of far more sins, and in countless cases it is in itself sinful.   The mere fact that an evil exists or recurs can never satisfy the Christian conscience.

People even go further and say because of the friendliness of our Lord Himself, and St. John the Baptist, and St. Paul with soldiers, that the Gospel cannot be the friend of soldiers, and the enemy of war.   We might as well say that the Gospel could not be the friend of sinners and enemy of sin.   Christ always makes this difference between person and thing, between sinner and sin.   He condemns the sin and pities the sinner. We ourselves are perpetually in the same position. The socialist curses capitalism and blesses the individual capitalist, a pacifist may be the sternest opponent of everything military and yet his dearest friend is a soldier.   How can people draw the conclusion that because St. John the Baptist and our Lord and St. Paul did not insist on soldiers giving up their profession, they approved of war.   Do not Christians, priests and religious, come daily in contact with those whose outlook and manner of life they disapprove, without thinking it necessary to expound their errors to them ? Christ, St. John and St. Paul do not say a word against their heathen religion to the Roman soldiers—but they do not, therefore, approve of it.   The Gospel method of conversion is always tender.   Its spirit works slowly, like leaven, in the Jewish and heathen masses, and only looks for error and imperfection to be got rid of very slowly.   But in fact this friendly intercourse of Christ and His followers—with *foreign* soldiers (and this should be noticed)—is directly opposed to the war spirit, for it shows us that they were quite free from nationalism.

We must not make the common mistake, made by those who wish to justify war, of pressing the letter, or some illustration, quite unfairly in order to get the meaning we want. Certainly this would be easier for the enemy than for the friend of war. Anything can be " proved " from Scripture. Still, the spirit of the Gospel is plain enough—justice, love, peace, humility. Because that spirit is just, it cannot, in certain circumstances, forbid injustice being met and opposed by force. Radical Pacifism, or the anarchical quietism of Tolstoi, which denies this right to use force, would become a Gospel of thieving and murder if any State adopted it. It is absolutely discredited by the Gospel account of the cleansing of the Temple when our Lord used physical force to drive out the buyers and sellers, and overthrew the tables of the money changers. He said to those who sold doves : " Make not My Father's House a den of thieves." We are told that His Disciples remembered the text, " The zeal of Thine House has eaten me up " (John II., 14–17). Christ's words, " But you shall not withstand evildoers " (St. Matt. V., 39) must not be taken as accepting injustice patiently. It is quite true that He forbids the Old Testament's eye for an eye, tooth for a tooth—the idea that we have a *right* to revenge, to the requital of evil with evil. The meaning of His command to Christians is : You must not withstand evil with evil, but, contrary-wise as I do, with good. The renunciation of this right of resistance really affects the private individual when he is unjustly accused and suffering is brought on himself alone. It is always a Christian's duty to see that when he defends himself against wrong he does not do wrong himself. If war could be carried on in the spirit of Christ in the Temple, with that consuming zeal for God's Honour, as God's Helper, as the executor of justice on evildoers (Rom. XIII., 4 ; St. Thom. 11, IIae 40, 1), then it would be justified before the judgment bar of the Gospel, but then only.

Common sense tells us that the *just cause* for war must be more than mere *material guilt*. The Gospel idea of justice is a higher and deeper idea than that of the Old Testament. To Christians and therefore to Christian politicians, statesmen, soldiers and generals, Christ says : " Unless your justice exceed the justice of Scribes and Pharisees you cannot enter the Kingdom of Heaven. You have heard that it was said of old ' thou shalt not kill. Whoso killeth shall be in danger of the judgment,' but I say unto you, whoso is angry against his brother, whoso calls him *Raca* is in danger of the judgment, but whoso calls him *thou fool* (one who forgets God, *Gottvergessener*) shall be in danger of Hell fire " (St. Matt. V., 20–22).

That is the judgment of Christ. It is deep and stern, and searches the heart and forbids not only the unjust deed, but the unjust feeling.

If this is the Gospel spirit how can we imagine that it gives its approval to war ? So far we have only thought of the justice of the Gospel, not its Love, which expects us to love our enemies ! Love them always ! Before war, during war, after war : " You had heard that it has been said to them of old time, thou shalt love thine enemy, do good to those that hate you, pray for those who despitefully use you and persecute you. For if you only love those who love you, what praise have you ? Do not the heathen do likewise ? Be ye also perfect as your Father in Heaven is perfect " (St. Matt. V., 43).

People who want to be good Christians and also good citizens of this world are perplexed by such words as these—their religious and worldly duties seem in honourable, but painful, conflict. A great breadth of mind and heart is indeed necessary if we are to understand them and their results. All the sects are wanting in this breadth. Their very existence depends on this one-sidedness. Their vision is limited to one side, almost to one word of the Gospel teaching. There is only one truth, generally only part of a truth, in this one-sided view, and therein lies their strength and their weakness. Their strength, because all their thought and striving and toiling is fixed on one point. Their weakness, because they must miss a universal outlook.

Those sects which condemn war always, and under any conditions, see in the Gospel only love and patience and peace, only the Christ who is meek and lowly of Heart and Who suffers wrong willingly. When they are confronted with the stern cleansing of the Temple, they are reduced to some such explanation as this: " because the Lord Jesus, when He cleansed the Temple, made a scourge of cords, does not prove that He used it, or that the traders were frightened by it. It was only a manifestation of divine peace to which they had to yield. The scourge may have been used to drive out the cattle " (John Horch).

Equally they pass over the solemn warning of St. Paul that the powers that be are ordained by God, for the terror of the evildoers, and that they are not to wield the sword in vain, but are to use it in the Name of God against evildoers. (Rom. XIII., 4.)

They emphasise the love of the Gospel so much that they forget the justice. The Gospel is wide as God Himself circled with the greatest mercy and the greatest justice, with Heaven and Hell. Justice, strength, sternness, the avoiding and the punishing of wrong must and shall remain. This is the answer to those who so misunderstand the teaching of Christ about Love— even to loving our enemies—and making His Teaching useless in real life, especially in the life of the State.

On the other hand we must not lessen the Gospel command of love, any more than that of justice. Evangelical justice is the application of force, free from any sinful passion, from hate, or love of strife, love of vengeance, or greed of possessions, and except in most rare and unusual cases it falls back on spiritual methods instead of force ; and here we must say a word to those who do not really grasp the Gospel spirit. They undervalue its real strength and power. They believe that hardness in life, and of men to each other wins the day over love and spiritual methods. The fate of Christ and the martyrs proves it. The fate of Christ and His true Disciples proves exactly the contrary. Those spiritual weapons of love, handled by Jesus and His followers, are incomparably sharper and more powerful than the arms of any warring power. This or that political kingdom has been set up by the sword, and there, surely, through its own sword or the enemy's, it has been by degrees weakened, and at last overcome.

Through the sword, things remain as they were. The benefits that come through the sword are no real benefits which can satisfy man's higher needs, only spirituality and love give us such benefits. They really build up the world, and the progress of true culture (which is something different from civilisation) is only possible when we have the spirit of peace and love.

The path of that spirit is often through suffering, as with Christ and the martyrs, but at last comes triumph, the triumph of the spirit of love.

Unfortunately the politicians of no State have tried the methods of Evangelical justice and love : that State would indeed be the greatest and most wonderful in the world. The ideal may not be realised till the millenium, but the Christian conscience must always have before it the ideal of the justice and the love of Christ even if it is never to be realised.

The over-ruling of wars is assuredly the most urgent need of any really Christian policy. Take any of the causes of war in the course of history and measure them under the Eye of Christ. The provocation may have been great, but would He have authorised the aggrieved State by its declaration of war to send millions of men to their death ? Should any king or minister or politician, calling himself a Christian—a Disciple of Christ— decide differently in any *casus belli* to his Master, Christ ? This is the only question which concerns Christians. The Christian who has different standards of justice for political and for private life differs from Christ. For Him there is no double standard of justice, no political interest alongside of the religious interest. Politics must be religious. The solution we are seeking is not indeed " Peace at any price," but " Justice at any price." But it is the justice of Christ which pursues murder and any hatred and bitterness unrelentingly. War undertaken for any other object than from zeal for the justice of Christ, which means the moral order announced and exacted by Him, is not to be accepted by the Christian conscience. If this object, which alone is allowable, cannot be attained by the world as it is to-day, then war loses any right to be, and loses that right far more before the bar of the Gospel than before that of the Law of Nature.

CHAPTER IV

THEORIES OF PEACE

A. IN THE PAST
    (1) OUTSIDE THE CHURCH
    (2) WITHIN THE CHURCH

B. IN THE PRESENT
    (1) OUTSIDE THE CHURCH
        (a) Classic Pacifism
        (b) Religious Pacifism
        (c) Young Pacifism
    (2) WITHIN THE CHURCH

THEORIES OF PEACE

A. IN THE PAST
(1) OUTSIDE THE CHURCH

PROTESTS against war are as old as war itself. As often as a father or a child or a wife or a friend stood beside the dead body of one who had fallen, the grief was natural and inevitable, the pride over the heroic death came later and was something exoteric. Added to the pain was the question as to the meaning of this violent death, of these countless deaths through the hands of fellow men. These questions were specially asked when the loved one who had fallen belonged to the conquered side. What was the sense of the sacrifice when it had encouraged the wrong instead of defeating it? If war made all the circumstances worse and victory was only a sign of the triumph, not of justice and right, but of brute force? There was an answer to these questions : the necessity for war which lay concealed somewhere in the nation's life : the failure of any earthly tribunal to judge between the nations as the result of the right of self-defence. But there remained the feeling that things were amiss, and the longing that they might be different. The older countries were the most ready to abstain from war. Not only weakness but also the tremendous cleavage between the various races of the existing world made it very difficult to imagine the possibility of any peaceful settlement between nations, which could take the place of war.   The foreigner was an unknown quantity against whom it was necessary to be on the watch.   Only the knowledge that in foreign countries men like themselves were dwelling, whose friendship would be an advantage, led to alliances and treaties.   The more the horizon was enlarged, the more the common spirit of humanity was recognised and the brotherhood of man emphasised, the more the mutual need and benefit of friendly relationship was realised, so much the more did Peace came to be desired.   We shall consider later the thoughts of Peace of the Chosen People.   As with the Jews so with the heathen, the greatest thinkers—as for instance, Plato, in his description of *Atlantis*—were critics of war, and to some extent, at any rate, Prophets of a Kingdom of Peace.

The first arrangement on record between two States is the Amphyctionic League which was instituted by Philip of Macedon for the decision of disputes between the various Greek Republics.   No less than eighty-one cases were decided by this court.*   By degrees this idea of a court decision made further progress, as wars and bloody feuds continued indefinitely ; yet when even Christian nations, in the middle ages, were involved, we see how slow the progress was towards civilised development.   Still the root idea that this state of affairs might be overcome by a mediator was ever more and more emphasised.   Augustine speaks of it in his *Civitas Dei*, Dante in his *Monarchia*.   These were indeed only propositions, not practical solutions.   The first practical suggestion for stemming the everlasting state of feud was the Pope's *Treuga Dei*—the truce of God.   With a certain mediaeval naiveté it decreed that from Wednesday to Monday in each week

---

* A. Raeder.   *L'Arbitrage international chez les Hellènes*, Christiania, 1912.

arms should be laid down. The feuds were, however, only really restrained by the introduction of the " eternal world's peace " of Maximilian I. at the Diet of Worms, in 1495.

A court of law took the place of armed self-defence.

This was a modest, but typical, step on the road to a universal court of justice.

Henry IV., in the sixteenth century, seems to have made the first political attempt towards a European union to promote Peace. In his *Mémoires des sages et sociales économics d'états*, published by his Minister, Sully, he propounds a plan for uniting Europe in a Christian Republic of fifteen States equally powerful. At the head of this alliance of States (which was to be made up of six hereditary sovereigns, six elected monarchies and three republics) was to be a General Council, composed of sixty representatives. Everything was carefully laid down, the boundaries of the countries, the number of soldiers, horses, cannon and ships, and the taxation. The object of the plan was an enduring armed peace among all European States. Henry IV. was murdered, and so the plan came to nothing ; but in any case the times were not ripe in Europe for such an alliance of States. That thinker was better advised who tried to work out a plan of the Law of Nations, according to the idea of the age. Hugo de Groot (Grotius) was considered the Father of the Law of Nations. Before him, however, the Dominican Francis de Victoria and the Jesuit, Suarez, had done good work. They only concerned themselves with the moral and theological, not with the practical side of the problem. This was left to Grotius who, in his celebrated book, *De jure belli et pacis* (1624), demanded an international court of decision. The Calabrian Dominican, Thomaso Campanella (1568–1639), wished for a universal monarchy under the guidance of the Holy See. A German Prince, Landgraf Ernst von Hessen-Rheinfels, a few years later, made a similar suggestion. Realising that in Catholicism, because of its stern discipline and its oneness of thought all the world over, lay the best hope for peace and unity, he proposed an alliance of all Catholic Princes. Disputes were to be settled by a court stationed at Luzern, a town especially suitable, since it lies between the two great powers, France and Austria. This idea of a union of all Catholic States, whose authority could not be disputed, is so striking that even now *mutatis mutandis* it is well worth consideration. Catholic politicians would, to-day, take the place of Catholic Princes. It would be a Catholic branch of the " inter-parliamentary union." Samuel Pufendorf (1632–1694) and Christian Thomasius (1655–1728) were the next supporters of the court of decision. Then came the French Carmelite, Emeric Crucé, whose book, *Le Nouveau Cynée* (1623), contains the earliest completed plan of a world-wide organisation, which should assure the independence of single States. This alliance was also to embrace States outside Europe, and Crucé was a forerunner of the modern Pacifist free traders. His warning to Princes is well worth considering. He tells them to beware of their military advisers and not to seek honour that is bought by bloodshed. The great French Archbishop Fénelon's name figures amongst Pacifists (1651–1715). Alfred Fried says of him : "He is the first Pacifist on the threshold of the eighteenth century who denounces war, except for defence, uncompromisingly. Between theft and conquest he sees no difference. Every war, even if it ends happily, does more harm than good in his opinion. He says in his *Télémaque*, ' The nations of the earth are all one family and instead of tearing one another to pieces, like wild beasts, they should form one great alliance in a Congress of all rulers.' " Fénelon's countrymen, Pascal, Boileau, La Bruyére, Pierre Bayle, all protested against war. It is wonderful how many Frenchmen have been amongst the most distinguished friends of Peace. One of the most celebrated was the Catholic priest, Charles Iréné Castel de St. Pierre (1658–1743). His *Project de la paix perpetuelle* (3 vols.) has occupied a distinguished place in political literature. Rousseau and Leibnitz supported his idea of a common European Army which was to keep order, but Leibnitz realised how difficult it would be for hereditary Princes to join any such project. In his letter to the Author, Leibnitz says that not until his death-bed, and then only if he left no family behind him, could any Minister support it. Voltaire mocked at the idea, but he also ridiculed those who say that pestilence, famine and war are all equally unavoidable. That is true of the two first, he says, " but war is made by man, by three or four hundred persons who rule the world, and whom we honour as Princes or Ministers." With equal truth David Hune compares those who instigate to war to drunken clowns who beat one another in a china shop and then have to pay a large bill. The French Encyclopedists were strongly opposed to war theoretically, but practically they were no friends of Peace as they prepared the ground for the brutalities of the revolution.

The plans of those who would improve the world by force were reduced *ad adsurdum* by the Revolution, by the rule of the masses and the dictatorship of Napoleon. Then came Immanuel Kant. This destructive abstract thinker took the question out of practical politics and propounded the idea of a peaceful State " in itself." His philosophical sketch, *Zum ewigen Frieden* (towards everlasting Peace), published in 1795, will always remain a classic of Pacifism. It is certainly no light *argumentum ex auctoritate* when a thinker like Kant considers the question of Peace worthy of serious consideration and then solves it in a positive sense ; we may disagree with Kant's philosophy, with his *Critic of Pure Reason*, and his religious and ethical opinions, but he cannot be belittled.   The title, " Everlasting Peace," is misleading, but the sketch itself is not at all utopian.   Cuno Fischer describes it truly : " It is quite free from sentiment or weak philanthropy, which were not at all Kant's characteristics.   He distinguishes very strikingly between sentiment and enthusiasm.   It was justice he loved so passionately because he understood it so well, and justice is not philanthropic, still less is it sentimental."

One thing Kant would never allow : that justice was utopian.   He believed in " *fiat justitia et pereat mundus* " and translated the words : Let right be done, even if all the rogues in the world perish.   Kant's realism proceeds from the supposition that " Peace between people living side by side is not the natural state (*Status naturalis*) " : it is far more a state of war, though not perhaps in the sense that Hobbes gives to it. Peace must therefore be built on the dominion of mind and morals over simple nature.   Certainly Kant says most strongly that nature in no way compels to war, but demands Peace and Repose.   Later Bismarck objected that only a State made up of angels would be influenced in its relationship with other States more by right than by might and self-interest.   Kant answers this objection by saying that in the organisation of a State within itself, and with other States, its members, even if they are not morally good, still may be coerced into being good citizens.   " We can see this in existing States which, though still insufficiently organised, subscribe to ideas of justice as far as may be, though true morality is certainly not the reason of their doing so."

All Kant's conditions for an enduring Peace are capable of development and improvement. For instance, he demands that standing armies should, by degrees, come to an end. " No State in time of war [so we see that he did not anticipate the immediate end of wars] shall be guilty of such actions as would make mutual confidence impossible when Peace is restored." Kant sees, in the development of oligarchical forms of government into purely democratic, actual grounds for the ending of war. As long as one man or a small group controls the destinies of a people, war will be lightly undertaken, like a game of chance. " If, however, the decision of the citizens were necessary, it is only natural that, as they have to bear all the burden of war, they should hesitate a long time before commencing anything so terrible " : therefore, in Kant's opinion, war is far less likely under a Republic than under a Monarchy. His ideal would be for all the individual States to combine, renouncing all their former aggressiveness, and so gradually all nations of the earth would be made one. But as at present they will not give up their rights as individual States, this dream of a world-wide Republic can only act negatively by warding off war and extending this bond of fellowship. Kant therefore has to be content with an *alliance* of nations, not a complete *union*, not a State made up of all peoples, but only this alliance which watches as much over national as international interests. The whole book displays great progressive idealism and wide realism, but it had little practical influence as the world was not ready for it.

A whole company of learned followers saw to it that his ideas should not be forgotten, and a whole school in France and Germany followed him. Jean Paul wrote vehemently against war : " The misfortune of war," he says, " is that two persons determine on it and millions carry it out. It would be much better if

millions made the decision and the two fought." Even
Johann Gottlieb Fichte supported Kant's teaching in
his early days, and when he preached a war of deliverance in his *Talks to the German Nation*, he considered
it as a forward step compared to the wars manoeuvred
by Cabinets, and looked on the people's war, which was
then going on, as the path that would lead to the united
Christian State.   After the Napoleonic wars even Napoleon himself, and the other Princes, seem to have
realised some sense of the responsibility for the Peace of
the nations which depended on them.   We have the
proof of this in " the Holy Alliance," in which the
Monarchs of Russia, Prussia and Austria pledged
themselves to rule only according to the precepts of
" Justice, Christian Love and Peace," and Napoleon
expressed still stronger sentiments from St. Helena.

According to Las Casas he said : " The Peace of Mos-
cow would have ended my wars and been the beginning
of security.   A new horizon, new aims filled with beauty
and prosperity, would have been revealed.

" The European system would have been established,
and, what mattered more, would have been organised.   I
too would have had my Congress and my Holy Alliance.
These ideas were stolen from me. . . . The task of
the century would have been accomplished, the Revolution perfected.   All that had not been disturbed was to
be improved.   It was my appointed task.   I had long
been preparing it—perhaps it would have cost me my
popularity, but that was immaterial.   I would have
been the bridge between the old and the new Covenant,
the natural mediator between the old and the new order
of things."

·   ·   ·   ·   ·

However well-meant and helpful these Peace plans of
princes and philosophers may be, war can only be

overcome by the people themselves. They have to
pay its awful price and they alone can break this scourge.
Theories of Peace and struggles for Peace must be made
popular if they are to have any effect. Though the
process is very slow, still the teaching of philosophers
against war is percolating more and more down to the
masses. Many false ideas come from above and work
down in their inexorable consequences.

So it was with the leaders of the French Revolution.
What Newman said about religious heresies—that
they always live by the remnant of positive Truth which
they contain and not by the negative falsehood which
will eventually work their destruction—is true also of
political heresies. Even the French Revolution stood
for certain truths and rights, namely the old truth of
the brotherhood of man which had been forgotten in
political and social life. The Revolution, of course,
distorted and corrupted it, but still by the Revolution
the truth was dragged out and shown noisily to the
world and it could no longer be ignored. The ideal of
Peace is inseparable from the thought of the brotherhood
of man. It becomes more and more the common
property of whole groups, whereas, as we have seen, it
was confined formerly to individuals. It is also the
reaction against reckless bloodshed, and so it came
about that the civil interest contested with the military
ever more and more for the foremost place. As military
power grew, so also did the protest against it—not only
in the heads of individuals but in whole groups.
The first organised anti-war protest of modern times we
owe to the English and American Quakers. On the
non-religious side, Dr. Worchester's book, *Investiga-
tions on War*, made a great stir (1815). After that
came the first Peace Societies in various countries.
Independently of any other, a Peace Society was founded
in London and six years later in Paris—the anti-war

" Society of Christian Morality "—and in 1830 came a similar movement in Geneva.

The first united attempt to influence world politics practically dates from a Congress in London of English, French and American delegates. All the civilised States were petitioned to accept an article in all international treaties which laid on all the powers the obligation, in case of a misunderstanding, of submitting to the mediation of one or other friendly State. The King of the French, Louis Philippe, said to the delegates : " Peace is necessary for us all and war brings so much suffering that one cannot lightly have recourse to it. Personally I am convinced that the day will come when it will have vanished out of the world." In those years (1810–1879) there was a simple American citizen who, from being a blacksmith, attained a high level of education and became an ardent Apostle of Peace —Elihu Burrit by name. He not only stirred the masses in England and America by his speeches, but he succeeded in convening two Congresses, one in Brussels, the other in Paris. At the latter he made urgent appeals to the Press and to the spiritual authorities. Thus gradually the Peace movement became more and more a people's movement. In older days monarchs could afford to discount public opinion because the people were politically dumb, but the more power came into their hands so much the more politics had to consider the interests and opinions of the masses, and they, in their deepest soul, became more and more opposed to war.

An imposing international Peace Congress was held in Paris in August, 1849, with Victor Hugo as Vice-President and the Archbishop of Paris as President. There were 23 delegates from the United States, two of them freed slaves ; England sent 800, France 250, Belgium 23 ; from Germany came Dr. Carové, of

Heidelberg, and Frederick Bodenstedt, from Berlin. Many other German Professors wrote expressing sympathy. Victor Hugo formulated the creed of the Congress in these words : " The day will come when arms will have dropped from your hands and war will appear as absurd between London and Paris, Petersburg and Berlin, as it would now be unthinkable between Basle and Zürich, or Glarus and Schwyz. The day will come when the nations of Europe will be as closely united as the Cantons are to-day in our Switzerland, and that without losing their individuality. The day will come when the only battlefields will be the markets of the world which will be opened not only to trading, but also to thought. The day will come when the place of shells and bombs will be taken by the voice and the common choice of the people ; by the Peace Court of a great sovereign Senate which will be for Europe what her Parliament is for England, the Reichstag for Germany, and the meeting of Cantons (the Bundesversammlungen) for Switzerland. The day will come when we shall see cannon only in museums, as to-day we see racks and instruments of torture, and wonder how such things were possible."

The third international Peace Congress took place the next year at Frankfurt a/Maine. Germany was again weakly represented, but the message of one of her greatest intellects, Alexander von Humboldt is most noteworthy. He wrote to the Congress : " Past history teaches us how, under the wing of a higher Power, there is in the life of the nations a yearning after a nobler end which will at last be satisfied."

The growing dislike to war found expression in an announcement made by the Catholic-conservative *Ligue internationale et permanente de la paix* (founded in Paris in 1867), by Frederic Passy, at its Paris Congress in 1869 : " Justification of war is a challenge to the common conscience. The new powers which have arisen are far more opposed to war than was formerly the case—these powers are industries and political freedom. The enormous proportion of the inhabitants of Europe wish for Peace and still, against her own interest, Europe finds herself under arms. The only cure for this state of things seems to be a closer and more comprehensive fellowship between men, and a political union like that of the United States."

Alongside the Catholic organisation, a free thinking " Lique internationale de la paix et de la liberté " sprang up in the same year at Geneva, which soon boasted of 60,000 members. In Germany, in 1869, a remarkable suggestion was brought forward by the free thinking leader, Rudolf Virchow : " Considering that the task of the North German Alliance (*Bund*) is directed principally by military authority and that the condition of readiness for war is supported in almost all European countries, not by the mass of the people, but by the Cabinets of the said States, the Government is requested to do all in its power through its diplomacy to hasten general disarmament." All these attempts fell far short of the goal.

Ten steps forward were counteracted by nine backwards, but the one remained : not only did wars become more rare, but the common conscience was more and more keen against the foolish and immoral spirit of War. The Geneva Convention of 1864—improved upon in 1867—is a proof, for by it hospitals for the wounded and all those dealing with sanitary questions were put under the international protection of the Red Cross organisation.

The French and German war of 1870–71 came as a great throw-back, from the standpoint of culture and humanity.

The terms of Peace contained the germ of more

misunderstanding between the two countries. They were prepared with unheard-of cynicism on both sides. Peace meetings certainly were held, and a great international Congress, in which Frederic Passy again took a leading part ; but the people were not behind him. The French paid homage to militarism in the hope of winning back what they had lost—the Germans from fear of losing what they had won.   In such ground the seeds of Peace could not take root, but political idealism cannot quite die out.   In defeated France the pacifist association, " La paix par le droit," was created in 1887 by French students.   Still more striking is it that in the following year, also in France, a powerful organisation of all the Peace Societies was inaugurated.   Nine English and twenty-five French members of Parliament determined, in October, 1888, to hold regular Conferences in Paris, and laid the foundation of the inter-parliamentary union.   After meetings in London, Bonn and Berne, this union became the Inter-Parliamentary Bureau, the headquarters of organised Pacifism, and established at Berne.   There were movements also in Germany.   It was the German character—not intellectual or power of organisation—that led the Peace movement.   A woman was at its head, Berta von Suttner.   Her novel, *Down with Arms of War* (*Die waffen nieder*), for the first time in Germany, tore the halo from war and with marvellous courage showed it in its true character as horrible and inhuman.

The novel appeared in 1890 and was translated into all the European languages.   It is sometimes too sentimental, and, because of its one-sidedness, not pleasant reading ; but the boldness and strength with which the reverse side of the shield is shown deserves all praise and is full of historic significance.   The book is epoch-making in its way, as was *Uncle Tom's Cabin* in the anti-slavery propaganda.   The following year,

Frau von Suttner founded the Austrian Peace Association, which was followed in a year by the German Association. In the same year H. Fried founded the first Pacifist periodical, taking the Suttner novel for its title.

The growth of the idea of a court of decision requires special consideration. Figures prove that during the last hundred years, in spite of the many wars, the desire of the nations has been to settle their disputes in a court of justice. Ten disputes were settled in this way during the years from 1821–1840; 25 from 1841–1860; 54 from 1861–1880; and 111 from 1881–1900. We must pass the years nearer the present day. One instance, however, may be mentioned as to the reception of these ideas in the German Parliament. At the suggestion of the Deputy, Dr. Barth, the following was put before the Reichstag in 1893 : " Whether the Government would support the endeavours of England and America to decide international disputes by a court of decision." On this occasion and also at a military debate of the same date the Centre Party was disposed to agree to the proposition. Dr. Leiber said : " It would be a great and beautiful task for the new age, a task greater than any earlier triumphs, if from the very soil which had been the scene of Bismark's rule of might a new rule of justice were to replace it and to spread over the whole of Europe." Two years later, in the Bavarian Chamber, Prince Lowenstein-Wertheim Rosenberg (who died a Dominican in 1921) pleaded for the erection of an international Tribunal to be " the consummation and crown of a system of justice which would respond to common sense, humanity and the Christian mind."

The universal Peace movement attained its greatest triumph in the two Hague Conferences. A manifesto of the Tzar of Russia in 1898 was directed against the ever-increasing jealousy of the great powers. It invited them to an international conference for the consideration of the question of disarmament. This conference took place at the Hague, in May, 1899. That systematic Pacifism is not utopian is proved by the fact that that party was the most doubtful as to the feasibility of the disarmament suggestions. To think of disarmaments was useless until an international court of justice was established which would replace the diminished armies. True Pacifism aims at an organised overcoming of the chaos of war from within, not from without. Disarmament would be no use if there were not an international court to take the place of armies, by which disputes would be settled in a statesmanlike manner.

The Conference went further than the merely negative consideration of disarmament, and determined certain questions of international justice. Laws were laid down in order to mitigate, wherever possible, the cruelty of war ; but the only real solution, namely compulsory investigation and the setting up of a court of decision to deal with disputed questions, was not brought forward. Not much more was done at the several Hague Conferences in 1907, chiefly because Germany would not agree ; but, nevertheless, the concrete influence of these conferences was undeniably towards the principles of Peace and acceptance of the fact that in a court of decision lay the only solution.

Idealistic endeavours to be of any use must have *real* support. The ruling powers and the rulers of science have such real influence. Both have been influenced by the Hague Conferences. The other power is money, and by degrees capital will be used to further the interests of Peace. Two notable examples are Alfred Nobel and Carnegie, both of whom left many millions for the furtherance of Peace.

(2) WITHIN THE CHURCH.

Christianity came into the world with the song : " Glory to God in the Highest and Peace to men on earth." Heaven and earth were to be one ; united through Him who stood between them, belonging to both ; reconciling both, uniting both in Himself, Jesus Christ, God and Man. As Very God of Very God, Christ could give the Father that Glory in the Highest which is His due, and as Very Man He could include all mankind among His brothers and sisters in His Divine Sacrifice of Praise, Thanksgiving and Reconciliation, and share with them the Peace, which flows from His union with His Father.

This was the task of the historic Christ, but He is the same, yesterday, to-day and for ever (Heb. XIII., 8) : what the historic Christ did and strove for, the Glorified Christ does and strives for at the Father's Right Hand in Heaven.

Further, as the Eucharistic Christ He comes down on earth as our companion, even as our Food so that He may be one with His own.

Again as the mystical Christ He is for ever with them in the one Body. As the Branches are one with the Vine, as the Head and the members, so for Him and for His People is it for ever true : " Glory to God in the Highest and on earth Peace." " To the men of His Grace " it is in the Greek. " To men of good will " in the Vulgate.

Here is the condition and the limitation of Peace. The Peace given and bequeathed by Christ is only the portion of such as are in the Grace of God and who are worthy, through their goodwill, of His Gift.

Man's acceptance of God's Grace is the condition, and his refusal, the limitation of this peace. Just according to the measure of the depth and reality with which the individual man accepts God, will he have much or little of His peace. And just according to the number of individuals who accept God's call of grace and peace, that peace is poured out upon them abundantly or is limited. In no other sense is Christ's peace limited. It is not an absolute peace like the peace of God and the Saints. It is not even an unclouded earthly peace, for it does not exclude sorrow and struggle. It is rather a hidden peace. *Something* within, and outside all life's changes, like a reflection on the soul of that Vision of God which Christ Himself always beheld, at work and at rest, in His journeys up and down the land and when He taught the people, when He prayed, and when He was reviled, on Thabor and before Pilate, at the Last Supper and on Calvary. Sometimes this peace of God which is beyond all earthly peace over-flows the house of the soul, the body, and shines out of the eyes like a light from Heaven. This peace, independent as it is of any earthly conditions, love of unrest and trouble, has little to do with political peace. Christ said : " My peace I give to you, not as the world giveth." Therefore it cannot be primarily the Church's business to further or to spread any other peace than this inner peace of the soul. The peace mission of the Church must always be considered, with this in mind. The Church's first and greatest task is the furtherance of God's Glory and the peace of Christ. This is done through the preaching of the Gospel, through spiritual and corporal works of mercy and through revealing the Secrets of God. If the ser-vants of the Church are sent to a chained and ill-used herd of slaves, or into the turmoil of battle, their first duty is not to save men's bodies, but to save their souls, not to bring about social and political peace but peace in the souls of men.

We must remember all this when we consider the

question of the world's peace from within the Church. It would be unjust and unscientific to make this question —the work of the Church and its results in resisting war —of primary importance. No doubt the work of political peace cannot be separated for long from the Church's Mission, but her first and most important work it is not and can never be. We do not begin to build a house from the roof, nor does a tree grow from its top branches down. We begin the house from its foundations and the tree grows from its roots. The foundation and root element of political peace always is, and always will be, the peace of individuals in their souls, in their relations to God and to their neighbour. There ought, indeed, to be a great division of labour in the work of bringing peace to the world. The State should care for political peace, the Church for the peace of souls. The kingdoms of the world ought to be thankful if the Church brought to them men who only possessed and cared for the peace of Christ. The nations might then build themselves a house in which there would be no more war.

But after all the Church must concern herself about political peace. Why ? Because practically it must be closely connected with the soul's peace. If God's Glory and the peace of Christ could be kept untouched, in war, as a drop of oil in water, if purity of soul and war were two elements which might touch but would not mix, then the Church might not concern herself about war, and might allow her members unconcernedly to approve it. But war is not a matter of moral indifference. It is closely allied to sin—indeed it is generally itself sinful—and those who take part in it are not, for the most part, especially in conscripted countries, outside the Church, but her members. They are Christians who are plunged into this sea of blood and hatred and revenge, members of the mystic Christ who destroy one another. Therefore the Church not only has an interest in war, but she shares in it.

This point of view did not concern the early Christians. They were in a small minority in the Roman Empire, and when a Christian was a soldier it was unlikely that he would fight against a Christian on the battlefield. But all the same war was allied to sin, and the Church had reason to fear that her children would lose, through war, not only their health and their life but also their souls. This was the negative side of her interest. War broke into her territory with sin in its wake. The positive side was the result of her thoughts of peace. She had only to concern herself with the spiritual peace of her children, but when this inner peace had spread, when the Kingdom of God had grown and Christ was more and more the Lord of the world, then the inner peace must of necessity reach out and at last a universal peace must be realised. This was not only in the inauguration, it was promised. Universal peace at the end of this dispensation and the beginning of the Messianic Kingdom was part of the Christian deposit of Faith. The first part of the promise was already fulfilled.

The time and place of the Messiah's birth, as told by Daniel, had come true, the plant from the root of Jesse had grown up, a Virgin had borne Emmanuel, the Spirit of Jehovah had rested upon Him, the Spirit of Wisdom and understanding, of counsel and strength. He had shown Himself the wonderful, the counsellor, the mighty God. Then, as was also prophesied, He was the Man of Sorrows and acquainted with grief. All these prophecies were fulfilled. His reign would also be accomplished, but when? That, no one could tell. " A King should reign in righteousness and the work of righteousness is peace and rest and safety for ever, and My People shall dwell in peace and safety " (Is.

H

XXXII.); "And the sword and war shall be no more and my People shall dwell in safety" (Hosea II.); "Then shall He judge the people and decide between many nations : and their swords shall be turned into ploughshares and no more shall nation draw their sword against nation, neither shall they learn war any more" (Is. II.).

The early Christians, especially their teachers, the Apostles, believed themselves to be in this Messianic time of peace. To enter into a new dispensation means to take the first steps, which involved in this case never letting out of sight the peaceful character of this Messianic Kingdom, and working patiently more and more for its realisation. Inner peace, as we have seen, must be the beginning—something great and new that Christ alone could give and which is His Messianic gift. The overcoming of war would only be considered last. To eliminate war from the world was not in the power of the early Christians. Solovieff says : "Historically Christianity, when it had been freed by the Peace of the Roman Empire, was not much concerned from day to day with the question of Peace or war. Christianity, of course, condemned absolutely all hatred and enmity, and on principle condemned war, but to cut the roots does not mean that the tree will fall directly, indeed the Gospel Messengers did not want it to fall at once because they knew the world was not ready. The seed of the true Faith was sown, but it would take time before it could grow from that seed, into the tree which should shelter both man and beast under its branches."

But had not the Apostles at least written against war and urged Christians to aim at its extinction ? That might have been the case—no doubt would have been— if they, and St. Paul in particular, had considered it necessary.

We must not forget that the Holy Scriptures, in spite of their absolute character, were, in one sense, opportunist, and undoubtedly in different circumstances certain things would have been written differently. What would St. Paul have written if he had been confronted with the spirit of modern war and many of its developments such as poison gas? Who can doubt that he would have used his scourge against such war? When he wrote, there were no wars, great or little, going on. He wrote under the Pax Romana. It was the day, not of political, but of religious nationalism. The Jews considered themselves, on account of their descent, better in the sight of God than Greek or Barbarian, and the Apostle opposed this nationalism.

As soon as Christendom had settled down into States and Christians were confronted, for the first time, with the problem of war, a great change began. The example of Christ, the Spirit of His Gospel, the Teaching of the Apostles, brought the early Christians up much more sharply, than is the case with us, against the contradiction between Christianity and war.

In some ways the contrast was more acute, for with military service idolatry was often intermixed. Soldiers, after a victory, had to assist with wreaths on their heads at sacrifices offered to a false god, or they had to take an oath of unconditional obedience to a heathen Emperor. Short of this, too, the bloody work of war seemed to many quite unfitting for the follower of Christ.

Tertullian, Origen and Lactantius were firm opponents of military service. Though Tertullian wrote his attack on military service (De Corona) when he was tainted with the Montanist heresy, we cannot say that he was in formal heresy on that account. Many true members of the Church, even martyrs, thought with him. Instead of condemning such an attitude of mind offhand, we may well consider whether it is not really much more in accordance with the spirit of the Gospel than the mental attitude which is most common to-day.

J. B. von Hirscher, speaking on the condemnation of war and of the military profession in the writings of many of the early Christians, says that it has its grounds in the inexhaustibly conciliatory spirit of Christianity and its willingness to bear wrongs, so that it cannot be said to be un-Christian.

Nevertheless Tertullian is too rigorous in many ways to be considered as a fair representative of Christian thought, as, for instance, when he forbids flight from persecution or second marriage, or giving the Holy Sacrament to those who had fallen into grievous sin. Origen, who was a much finer and nobler thinker, so spiritualised rude reality that, as we have seen, he considered the Old Testament wars as simply typical and allegorical. Celsus, a heathen, had accused the Christians of lacking patriotism, because they evaded military service. To this Origen answered that there was a higher patriotism " by which we overcome those devils who cause war and destroy Peace. We do our rulers better service than do those who bear the sword. Better than they do, we fight for the Emperor. Truly, we do not go with him into the battlefield, not even if he commands it, but we fight for him in our camp, a camp of Holiness wherein we pray to God."* Origen quoted St. Paul who says that the Christian warfare is not fleshly, but spiritual, and all Christ's disciples being Priests, they must not shed blood. Lactantius also speaks plainly against violence : " The just are not allowed to bear arms. Their service is justice—they may not even accuse a criminal for it is really all one

---

* *Contra Celsum,* VIII.

whether we slay a man with a sword or with our words. There is no exception to this Law of God."*

Though these extreme views were not those of the Church there was a very strong feeling against military service amongst the early Christians. "Did not Jesus," asks Harnack, "forbid all revenge and retaliation for wrong endured? Did He not teach only gentleness and patience? Were not soldiers despised for their violence? (In those days the police service was done by soldiers and that often brought them into bad odour.) Therefore," he said, " undoubtedly a Christian ought not willingly to be a soldier. It was not difficult to evade service, for there was no conscription in the Roman Empire—the fact was just this : the baptised Christian did not become a soldier."†

Athanasius describes the tremendous change which the conversion of the Greeks and barbarians made in their conduct : " These men, who could not live an hour without weapons of war, have given them up since they became Christians, and have taken instead to the plough ; and their hands, which hitherto wielded the sword, are raised to Heaven in prayer. Instead of war, which they waged against one another, they now fight against the devil for the cause of virtue and purity of soul. Those who understand the Law of Christ fight against temptation and their weapons are their virtues and the purity of their morals."‡ Many even died the martyr's death rather than become soldiers, as, for instance, St. Maximilian, the son of the old Legionary, who, when he was commanded to join the army, refused saying that as he was a Christian it was

---

* *De div. institut cap.*, VI., 18 and 20.

† *Militia Christi, Die christliche Religion und der Soldatenstand in den ersten 3 Jahrhunderten,* Tübingen, 1905.

‡ *De Incarnatione,* Migne P. G., 25, col. 185.

not allowed. He was beheaded in consequence in 295 A.D.

Probably SS. Victricius and Paul are similar cases. St. Martin remained in the army two years out of love for his captain, then he laid down his arms, saying that in future he would only be a soldier of Christ.* There were numberless Catechumens in the army, but after baptism they generally left. Some who stayed on after Baptism received the martyr's crown.

The Church has never forbidden military service as such. Tertullian ceased to be a Catholic and even Origen and Lactantius are not authoritative, but the spirit of the Church was undoubtedly opposed to war and all its work. This is proved by what has just been stated, and by the writings of Catholic and holy men such as Cyprian, Chrysostom and Ambrose. They were not so severe as Tertullian or Origen or Lactantius, but whoever reads their works will see what they thought and what they expected from their brethren in the faith. St. Cyprian says that war is cursed a thousand-fold by the people : " Murder is a crime if it is committed by one man, but it is honoured as virtue and bravery in the mass. Therefore it is not innocence which. goes unpunished but an enormous crime."† These are the words of a man of whom Joseph Wittig, on the authority of St. Augustine, says : " Many Bishops there were, but he was called *The* Bishop. Many teachers, but they were for their own country, their own time, their own Church. Cyprian was the teacher of all Christendom, of the Universal Church of the ages."‡

" Cyprian's writings," says Bardenhewer, " are so highly esteemed that they are looked upon as part of

---

* *Acta Sanctorum,* Oct., *t,* XII., p. 531.
† *Ad Don.* 6.   ‡ Wittig. Wiedergeburt, 1923.

revelation and have received almost canonical authority. His words on war, calling it murder and crime, coming from the best times of Christianity, carry weight."*
St. Chrysostom also preached from the Gospel heights which are so far above this world's standard. " No one must do his neighbour a wrong or meet injustice with injustice, but wrong must be willingly endured, nor must we hate the wrongdoer—rather must we love him, do him good and pray for him."†

St. Ambrose says : " Those who would live after the Gospel ask not for revenge. They leave it to Him who has said : ' Vengeance is Mine.' It is unfitting for Christians to pay back evil for evil."‡

" Not evil with evil " ; but to oppose, with all one's strength, good to evil. That is a hard saying and because of it the Church could not be an absolute enemy of war. St. Ambrose rightly tells us that " the valour which protects our country by war against the barbarians and protects the weak, this valour is full of justice," § and this view is pre-eminently right. After Christianity had been acknowledged as the State religion by Constantine, there was no danger of Christian soldiers being forced into any heathen observances. We must never forget, too, that the wars of the late Roman Empire were technically, at least, much more justifiable on the plea of justice than the wars of to-day. They were either undertaken against a rebellious province or in self-defence, against the inroads of barbarians. Such undertakings could be most justifiable. The Church had a moral interest in them, because the existence of the Church and the State were

---

* *Bardenhewer : Geschichte der altkirchlichen Literatur*, Band 2,2. Auflage.

† *Hom.*, XVIII. *In cap., v. Matth.*   ‡ *Chron. Matth*, V.
§ *De Offic.* I. 1. c. 27.

both threatened by these attacks against the Empire, and against Christianity.

Necessity and justice alone can render war excusable. It is wrong to love war for its own sake, though people are inspired by it as if it were something ideal, and they *fete* it as such. We find no trace of such a spirit in the Christian writers of olden times. This glorification of war and its deeds was quite unknown in the first and best days of the Faith. We find there no enthusiasm for it. The early Christians thought as Christ did about the Kingdom of this world. The State must exist and it is sad when it is broken up ; but after all what true Christian would break up with the State ? Christ is more above the State than in it. His Heart does not cling to civil or military display. So thought all those early Christians who were not limited by national restrictions. There were no Hymns in honour of war, and if there had been they would not have been on the lips of the Christians. " He who can think of war unmoved," says St. Augustine, " has lost all human feeling."* " Peace should be dearer to us than anything. There is no greater glory than to have kept Peace ; and glory, won through conquest, is despicable."† " It is more creditable to have killed war by our words than to kill men with the sword, to win Peace through Peace, not through war."‡

The shedding of blood matters more than the staining of body or soul. The Christian Church will not follow the Synagogue in this. " To kill in a just war," says Isidore of Pelusis, " is no sin, but why does Moses require that those who return from war should be purified ? I answer, because although it is permissible to kill your enemy in battle, and although we erect trium-

---

* *Civ. Dei*, LXIX., c. 7.   † *ibid*, I., III. c., 14.
‡ *Epist.* 229, c. 2.

phal arches for the victors and honour them, slaying in war is not free from blame when we think of the higher relation of man to man."* The German Benedictine, Abbot Rhabanus Maurus, of Fulda, afterwards Archbishop of Mainz (died 856), saw deep into the passions excited by war when he wrote to Bishop Herebald, the penitentiary : " Men say that none of the soldiers need do penance because they have obeyed their princes, but we must examine whether those who defend themselves against the guilt of murder are really so innocent in the Eyes of God : whether they have not been influenced by greed, or the wish to ingratiate themselves with their leaders, and so have disregarded the command of God, ' thou shalt not kill,' not accidentally, but on purpose."

In the early Church those who had killed even in a just war had to do penance. St. Basil writes : " Our Father did not class killing in battle as murder because those who fight for justice and right must be exonerated, but I should advise that *they should be kept from communion for three years* because their hands are stained with blood."† Vanderpol, who has gathered together the sayings of the Primitive Church on war,‡ says that St. Basil's opinion was not approved, but that the Bishops fell back on the canonical letter of their Metropolitan when the Emperor Phocas intimated to them that all soldiers fallen in war were to rank with the martyrs. The book of penance of St. Egbert, Archbishop of York (750), decrees a penance of forty days for anyone who has killed another. Abbot Reginos says the same in 915. The Council of Rheims (923) decreed a penance for all those who took part in the battle of Soissons between the Emperor Charles the

---

* *St. Isid. de Pel. Epist.*, 200, lib., IV. *Ophilio grammatico.*
† *Epistola canonica*, 245 *ad Amphilocium*, 13.
‡ *La doctrine scolastique du droit de guerre,* Paris, 1919.

Simple, and his adversary, Robert, the claimant to the throne, supported by Southern France. The war was considered as a war of Burghers (citizens) and penance was imposed on both parties. It consisted in being expelled from Church all through Lent, fasting on bread and water for several days in Lent and Advent, and lasted three years.*

That the conscience of the soldiers was in sympathy with the opinion of the mediaeval Theologians is proved by an occurrence in the time of William the Conqueror.

Certain of his men were in doubt as to the justice of his cause, and the deeds of violence perpetrated left their conscience no peace. They consulted their Bishop. A council assembled in Winchester in 1087 and drew up a list of penances which were approved by the Papal Legate. For every enemy killed, a year's penance ; for every one so badly wounded that the result was doubtful, forty days' penance ; if the soldier did not know how many he had killed or wounded he was to do penance one day a week for the rest of his life. Archers were not to shoot during three Lents.†

The whole practice of the Church is contained in the words " *Ecclesia abhorret a sanguine.*" This has certainly not prevented priests and bishops from taking active part in wars. No words can condemn such conduct too strongly, and this the official Church has always done. The Council of Toledo, in 400 A.D., degraded all priests whose hands were blood-stained, from their priestly office, and condemned them to life-long penance in a Cloister. " If a Priest," the same Council decreed, " is killed in war or in strife, no masses or prayers shall be said for him. Let him fall into the hands of his Judge. Only Christian burial shall be given him."‡

---

* *Mansi*, XVIII., 345–46.   † *Mansi*, XX., p. 459.
‡ *Decret. Grat. dist.* LI., c. 4 and 8.

Fulbert, Bishop of Chartres, who died in 1029, writes to St. Hildegard : " Churchmen who understand more about war than secular Princes, and who dare to disturb the Peace of the Church, and to shed the blood of Christians, should be called not bishops but tyrants." Pope Nicholas I. (858–867) had said " The Church knows only one sword, the sword of the spirit which does not kill but gives life."*

In the tenth and eleventh centuries when feuds were as frequent as trials by law are now, the Church did much to restrain them. The Truce of God, which forbade strife for the greater part of the week (from Wednesday evening till Monday morning), under the strictest laws of the Church, was a great step for the times and shows an essential wish for Peace in the Rulers of the Church.

But did not the Church herself take the sword in her hands in the Crusades ? This question cannot be passed over and must be met fairly.

What was the object of that mighty movement ? The conquest of the Holy Land for Christendom and the certainty of an open road to reach it. Was this a lawful object for war ? Was nothing else involved— quite certainly nothing else ? It is not permissible to gain a religious end, even the conversion of unbelievers or the gaining of religious property, by force of arms.

The middle ages were not disposed to accept this ruling. After Christ had come everyone was bound to believe in Him. As the King of Spain could coerce rebellious French subjects into obedience to their King, so could the Kings of the earth coerce the unbeliever into obedience to the Heavenly King.†

If Christ came on earth again, and whole nations despised Him, Christians would have the right to

---

* *Migne*, CLXI., p. 258.

fight for Him, and this held good after His death. Francis de Victoria answers (*De Indis*) that no unbeliever is guilty to whom the Gospel has not been preached, and even if Christianity had been put before him it would be careless and wrong of him to accept it off-hand before he was sure that the preacher was trustworthy and could show undeniable and legitimate proof. Therefore there was no justification for a war, and the unbelievers were innocent in these circumstances. A just war was only possible when it was waged against the morally guilty. Even if they were deaf to the most wonderful sermons accompanied by miracles, though they would be guilty in the sight of God, there would be no justification for war because no one can be forced to believe, as St. Thomas says, " Faith is an act of the will and fear weakens the will " (II., IIae., X. 8). Victoria had in mind the Spanish rule in America which was far worse than the Indian, and over which a mantle of religion had been thrown. They were guilty and not the wretched Indians !

Were the circumstances the same in the wars of the Christians in the East ? No, they were not, for the Mohammedans had persecuted the Christians for centuries. War was Islam's chief means of propaganda. It was an article of faith to fight against the unbeliever, a religious and political principle. The Saracens had overrun nearly the whole of Spain, and Sicily, Gaul and Italy were threatened. Many Christians were killed or injured, and especially in the Rhine valley and in the Alps, communications were intercepted.

What tried the Christians most, however, was the ill-usage of the Pilgrims to the Holy Land. Many never arrived at all, though they had wandered about and endured terrible sufferings. Many were enslaved. The most trustworthy eyewitnesses, like Peter the Hermit, were never weary of telling their experiences.

He rode on his donkey from place to place, describing them in glowing colours, and his personal holiness naturally increased the impression of his words. In this way an honourable excitement and movement were brought about, based on moral and religious motives. An imperial call for help from Constantinople set the seal on the numberless complaints and entreaties of the pilgrims, and so a state of mind was prepared into which Pope Urban II. had only to throw the en-kindling spark of inspiration for a Crusade—to protect the Christians and to win back the Holy Places.

It was always clear that the wish in any circum-stances to rescue the Holy Places from the Turk and to ensure liberty for the pilgrims in the future would lead to war.

The war seemed a just one. St. Bernard voiced the moral conscience of the age when he said : " Un-believers should not be punished with death if any other means would prevent their oppressing Christians, but this extreme measure was better than to allow the ill-treatment of just persons and so to share in the injustice."* The middle ages believed that war against Islam was always justified, even if there was no immediate cause. On this point the Catholics and Protestants of the sixteenth century were agreed. Guerrero (died 1587), the canonist, declares that " unbelievers who are peaceable must not be attacked without reason ; but others, like the Saracens, must be resisted even when they wish for Peace for we must always remember that if they had the opportunity they would attack the Christians. They fight against the whole world, and the whole world fights against them. They never keep the peace and therefore they are not to be con-sidered."† Sayings such as this must be judged in the

---

* *Migne,* CLXXXIV., C., 3.   † *De bello justo et injusto.*

light of the spirit of the times, and we must always remember that Islam's aim and object was the conquest of Christendom. If a man holds as a religious principle that he should root out and destroy anything he disagrees with, it is worse than elevating stealing and robbery into a principle of life and conduct. Only sectarian prejudice and blindness can maintain that in those days violence should have been met by passive resistance. To say so is to misunderstand existing circumstances completely. But the approval of armed opposition must be qualified by St. Bernard's words : " That there were no other means," and further, according to the teaching of the middle ages, there must be practical certainty that by war the evil would be rectified, and not made worse.

Standing, as we do, at a distance of many centuries from the Crusades, we can consider them dispassionately and whilst it is true that, theoretically, they were carried on under these two conditions, practically it is difficult to justify them.

It is really true that these wars, lasting for years were the only means for attaining the desired end ? That will certainly be doubted to-day, by Catholics as well as by others. This is Albert von Ruville's* opinion, and he is a great historian of the Catholic Church. He denies that at the time of the Crusades, war against the Saracens was really necessary. The danger of their supremacy was greatest in the eighth, ninth and tenth centuries. After that there was a strong Christian re-action, and by the beginning of the eleventh century the danger was practically over. It was then that the Crusades began, and they had much more the spirit of Israel in its old Kingly days than the spirit of their Divine Master.

---

* *Die Kreuzzuge*, Bonn and Leipzig, 1920.

The Christian could not exist without arms of war. Even Ecclesiastics of high rank went armed into battle, for they were of the secular Princes and considered that it was their duty to fight.

The strength and freshness of the German stock and its rough paganism, which the Church had not really overcome, made itself felt. Fighting and conquering were the ideals. The possibility of becoming a reigning Prince or, at any rate, a feudal Lord, was before every knight ; at least he could make sure of considerable booty. The Crusades were specially knightly undertakings. Ruville does not deny that Pope and Church encouraged the Crusades, and when they appeared justifiable, gave them the Church's blessing. He allows weighty grounds for the offensive, the winning back of stolen lands, and the old-established privileges of Christians in Palestine, the righting of many grievances by which worse dangers in the future were probably prevented : but that the spiritual power itself, the representative of the Prince of Princes, should organise the Crusades and carry them out, that he cannot approve. " It is astonishing that Christianity was never so near to Islam as when they fought most bitterly. The Popes behaved like the Khalifs in that both encouraged and led those ' Holy Wars.'

" The idea of winning Heaven through deeds of blood dominated both sides."

To judge motives and intentions is always dangerous, the tremendous idealism of the crusaders, which Ruville does not underrate, may have been purer than that of the Mohammedan, but the School the Christian had learnt in was far above the School of Islam.

We are more interested in the facts than in the good intentions. Even if both the good cause and just intention (*causa justa* and *intentio recta*) of the Crusades fulfilled the moral demands, even if they were necessary and defensive and not offensive, still they would not have been just wars according to those qualifications of morality and theology which we have already considered, if they failed to satisfy that standard in the past, the present, or the future. For such a terrible thing as war to be justified before the bar of common sense, of God and of man, before past generations and generations to come, the results must be worth the stake, that is the triumph of justice must be morally certain. Also it must be carried out according to Gospel precepts which are higher than material or Old Testament laws. In both points the Crusades failed. There was no question of that prudence and consideration of which our Lord tells us in the parable of the King, who, before he went to war, considered what his resources were (St. Luke XIV., 31). Short of a miracle—and to expect that would have been to tempt God—even an orderly arrival in the far-off Holy Land, was almost an impossibility. The hapless hordes of peasants who had no regular troops with them were simply aimless wanderers—and then the children's crusades. Were they not pure madness? For out of the seven ships of pilgrim children which left Marseilles, five sank before they reached Sardinia. The other two got to Alexandria where, with four hundred Priests, they were sold into slavery. A German children's pilgrimage had no better luck. The children died in masses, either of hunger or disease, and many girls suffered a worse fate. Victory for such an undertaking was anything but a moral certainty—rather a moral impossibility.

Further, as to the right way of conducting war by not over-stepping the limits of justice and love—or the inner and the external behaviour towards the enemy : the Crusaders' guilt in this respect was horrible. Even in the first Crusade, on the way to Palestine, when the ideals were still pure, the murdering of Jews and the conflagrations were hideous. When the Holy City was at last reached the Christian sword was lifted against everybody, even women and children, and the murder and plundering were endless. This was followed by going in procession in deep devotion to the Tomb of the Redeemer. Ruville says : " We ask in horror how the two can be combined—blind, indiscriminate murder and the undoubtedly real devotion and thanksgiving at the Holy Places. The explanation lies in the Old Testament influence on western Christendom. Latin Christianity considered itself almost the chosen people of God, who went to the Holy Land to free it from the heathen."

God's blessing did not rest on the Crusades. It was not just a mishap which might occur from material causes, but quite extraordinary disasters befell them. It was their greatest leaders, Conrad III., Frederick Barbarossa, Henry VI., Frederick II., who were struck down by illness, sudden death and other " accidents." " After fifteen years Jerusalem was taken. The object in itself must have been against God's plan, for every one who took part in it bit on stone—but the stone was not the enemy, it was the opposing will of God, which made use of a thousand material causes and circumstances." Ruville finds this will of God expressed in the proverb, " Jerusalem will be trodden down by the heathen till the times of the heathen are fulfilled." " Only when the great Missionary work is accomplished will Jerusalem cease to be trodden down by the heathen. Its inhabitants shall only be released from the heathen in the last days because they were unworthy, because they betrayed the Messiah."

One thing is certain, that God has worked differently from what man would have expected. The Crusades have occupied us at such length because they afford most interesting material for the consideration

I

of the problem of Peace and war and it would not be
possible to omit them in a chapter on "Theories of
peace within the Church in the past," for they are
a great counterproof of the Church's mission of
Peace.

Anyone who is acquainted with the spirit of both
Catholic and non-Catholic cultivated and ignorant
thought, knows how depressing it is when everything
to do with the Church is apologised for and justified.
We know what a relief it is when shadows are acknowledged to be shadows, stains to be stains, puzzles to be
puzzles. How much better it is to acknowledge and
bewail that the Catholics in practical daily life, lay people,
priests, bishops, popes, have, to a great extent, forgotten that the Church is the bearer of the Spirit and
the Office of Christ, the Mother of all mankind, the
Mystical Body of Christ, and that in the course of the
world's history her members have fallen short and still
fall short of her high calling. If this is acknowledged,
the Catholic ideal stands much higher and is much
purer. This ideal, as contained in the Church's teaching
on Faith and Morals, is unassailable, unanswerable and,
in all times, has been held by great and pure-minded
supporters, even during the Crusades and by the
Crusaders, as, for instance, Peter the Hermit, Bernard of
Clairveaux, St. Louis of France, all of whom were noble
members of the Mystical Body of Christ.

How deeply religious the ideals of many, probably
most of the Crusaders were, we can but measure if we
think what the strength of their Faith was. He who
embraced the Cross broke with his entire social life.
He left wife and child, house and home behind him
and went forth to face immense dangers and hardships
for his Redeemer's sake, and this was no duty, it was all
voluntary. Certainly it appealed to the spirit of adven-
ture and love of fighting, but it was also a work of Faith

and self-sacrifice, of which we, to-day, can have no conception. The leave-taking of the Landgraf of Hessen and Thüringia from his young wife, St. Elizabeth, must always be an affecting story. These two hearts, united in the tenderest, most precious, love, were torn asunder, and they brought their offering to Him whom they loved more than one another, their Saviour, Jesus Christ. There may not have been many such but they do credit to the Church because she it was who trained them.

The reproach that the Crusades were unsuccessful only touches one side of the Church and her task. Her task is to live for the Glory of God and to fight in the spirit of Christ, her Head. To promote zeal for God and to keep holy even His earthly Dwelling, Palestine, was a deed of noble love and piety. The mistake was in the way in which it was carried out, the cruel obstinacy in spite of endless proofs of its impossibility—flying in the face of facts for nearly two hundred years. The Crusades are, therefore, a standing example of what this book is written to prove—that the actual justice of a war (which is its only condition) does not seem to be arrived at even when the objects appear most undeniably in its favour. No wars in history since the Birth of Christ could seem more ideal as to object than the Crusades, and still even these wars were not really " just " according to the measure required by the Gospel of Christ and the Theology of the Church.

So much for principles. What were the results, in history, of the age of the Crusades which were the highest and most characteristic expression of the strength of mediaeval Christianity ? Was this age one of progress or of retrogression compared to the age preceding it ? We have seen what the Church thought about war in the eleventh century, when the Crusades

I—2

began ; how she considered bloodshed even in a just war as a stain from which it was necessary to be cleansed at any cost. It is indeed to be regretted that this ideal was lost during the Crusades, and it was certainly not progress. Perhaps in political influence and zeal for the Church as a spiritual power in the world, the age of the Crusades was an advance on the first thousand years after Christ. Science and art, too, progressed greatly, owing to the communication between East and West, which also enabled the Church to carry on her missionary work. " The Crusades were the school of the age of discovery and of the whole idea of modern colonisation with which missions have always gone hand in hand, to win the first place all the world over " (Ruville). The Church had grown out of the narrow boundary of the first thousand years, but we cannot say that she profited interiorly in consequence. It can truly be said of the Church : What does it profit her to win the whole world and lose her own soul. By which is meant the souls of her individual members, not, of course, the corporate soul of the Mystical Body of Christ. That soul is the Holy Ghost proceeding from the Father and the Son ; eternal as They are, the same yesterday and for ever. On the side of her temporal development and her human weakness the Church can be led astray. On the other side is her divine and absolute infallibility. Popes can err in matters that do not affect faith or morals, and assuredly taking the sword was a case in point. Further, so far as the Crusades punished the heavy guilt of the Turk and defended Christian interests, the Popes were justified in blessing them, but they should not have been the immediate aggressors organising the Crusades.

Not only were men killed, but their souls lost by the sword used against the Mohammedans. Whether this show of Christianity was responsible for saving anyone, it is impossible to tell. Such fruits are, at least, not visible.

In these days a Crusade would be impossible. Is this progress or the reverse? It would indeed be going back if the human race no longer had sufficient faith and self-sacrifice to endure the hardships and sufferings the Crusaders endured, for the sake of Christ and the Church. We may be inclined to deny such idealism to present-day Christianity and to doubt whether masses of men would be found to offer themselves for a work of Faith, if the Church were again to go to war for the attaining of some religious object. What are we to say as to the capacity of modern Christians to make great sacrifices for the faith? We believe that they would not fail—perhaps not in such large numbers and not in support of war, but perhaps for Peace? Supposing a new world war broke out and the Church were to forbid her members to take part in it, on the strength of the arguments of moral theology, and if this refusal to fight were punished by imprisonment and death, I believe that the religious self-sacrifice of numberless Christians would stand the test.

The Church, since the days of the Crusades, has never laid down any practical laws. She has left it to theology to develop gradually a theory as to war being allowable or not. This is not rooted in any very deep cause. Many things, such as riches or alcoholic drinks, are misused by the world, but the Church does not require total abstinence from them as long as they are used properly—not that war is to be compared to luxurious living or to intemperance, because it is always an evil, but it need not *necessarily* always be a moral evil on *both* sides and it may bring with it a remnant of what is indifferent or even good; and on account of this remnant, war is, at least theoretically, just within the boundary which separates things which are amoral (not right or wrong) from things which are immoral.

For this reason the Church has hitherto left each one
personally free to take military service.

We will see, later on, that the Church has the right to
limit this permission.

In the Kingdom of God progress is not only from the
Old to the New Testament, but also from an immature
Christianity, gradually developing to the full maturity
which is to be realisèd at the Messianic end of the world.

B. In the Present.

(1) Outside the Church.

Man, in the course of history, has had much experience of war. It was no phenomenon of nature like
storms and thunder. Still it broke over mankind
like an elemental, natural catastrophe over which he
had no control. It followed that in time, by observation
and experience, man learnt wisdom. Lightning con-
ductors and other means of protection were invented,
and so with war. The longer men were at its mercy,
the more they were compelled to search for its cause and
for its possible prevention. They gazed helplessly at
it, half in reverence, half in fear, but quite unable to
tackle its wild fury. Then gradually men arose, at
first only Thinkers and Poets ; but by degrees the
masses, who asked themselves whether they were
indeed quite helpless, whether there was no means of
overcoming this madness.

We have seen how always in history, parallel with the
lust of war, has been the growing lust of Peace—in its
infancy either small and weak, or else too bold, too
hurried and therefore of as little use as the most hesitat-
ing protest. Gradually this Peace movement became
more striking, more practical. " The first protests,"

says Johann von Block, " flowed from the heart of persons so penetrated by feelings of humanity that war was abominable to them. The appeal was to sentiment more than to reason, but this is always the fate of Ideals. They attract first, through their beauty, later through their truth, but when the ideal is established and is seen to have a future, it enters upon another phase. It is supported by knowledge and has a solid foundation of truth."*

Philosophical enlightenment is, however, not the last step through which an ideal passes on the way to full development. The ideal, purified and deepened by philosophy, must sink down again to the masses from which it originally came. This has been the developing process of the Peace Ideal. It remained for long in the region of sentiment and desire—only in the last hundred years has there been organised and systematic endeavour to reach the goal.

(a) CLASSIC PACIFISM

The result is called *Pacifism*. It is a belief of the mind and the heart, an acknowledgment, in word and deed, of conviction. Pacifism believes that disputes can be arranged by other means than international wars, if there is the will to find these means. There are various motives for this belief and various ways in which it may be realised, so that we have various kinds of Pacifism. We shall consider that which is, more or less, the origin of them all, and which we shall call *Classic* Pacifism, on account of its scientific basis and its quiet sanity. Classic Pacifism simplifies and condenses all the theories. Kant's theory was free of illusion and sentiment, but he called it " towards ever-

---

* *Der Krieg*, Band V., 527.

lasting Peace." No one would do so to-day. The word everlasting is misleading, and has quite disappeared from contemporary Pacifist terminology.

Alfred Fried, through whose writings the Peace movement has entered upon a completely new phase since the days of Berta von Suttner, says that modern Pacifism is as little concerned with the everlasting duration of Peace as is an engineer in the everlasting duration of a bridge.

We have only to consider the present generation. The next will find its own ways of improving and building up what we have begun. It is no question, as in the days of Kant, of distant aims and objectives, it is simply what is possible for to-day and to-morrow. This possibility depends on strenuous and scientific work for the undermining of war principles and the building up of Peace principles. Put shortly, *Classic Pacifism is the scientific and practical denial of the system of international rule of might, by an international system of the rule of right, of justice.* He is a Pacifist who accepts this programme without compromise. This is clear, but it is very far from the narrow one-sidedness so often called Pacifism.

Overcoming the international rule of might means scientific examination of all the complexes which make up war, including causes and results. Philosophy, medicine, history, statistics all come in. The introduction of a system of international justice includes knowledge of law and statecraft, of national economic ethics, education, politics. All this must be made simple in the propaganda by making popular the scientific knowledge and the aim in view.

This is modern Pacifism with its activities. It is obviously more capable of a scientific and ethical discovery of the causes of war (which must be its first duty) than any merely national means of investigation can be, because it is by nature supernational and less hampered by party spirit. As an example of scientific examination of the technical, social and political side of war and its consequences the Russian (Johann von Block's) book, *Der Krieg*, is surprisingly justified by the late World War. What everybody knows to-day— that because of the terrible loss of life, because of the waste of money, because of the exhaustion of all the nations—war is for both sides an immense misfortune, and that victory is not worth the price : all this von Block clearly foresaw fifteen years ago. He believed that *war, not Peace, would bring Utopia because,* on account of its horrors, its ruin to the individual and the State, it would bring about its own destruction. When science and experience have got so far, Pacifism can restrain itself from any violent tendencies in its work of enlightenment. It is satisfied to share in what are facts. There is still the other side. Outside Pacifist circles war is still looked on as the means of righting wrong, of restoring morality, order and honour, not as Klopstock calls it, " The loud scornful laughter of the deepest hell." Scientific Pacifism declares emphatically that its task lies less in the negation of war than in the positive creation of enduring principles of Peace. Alfred Fried inveighs against what he calls (not very happily) " Reform Pacifism,"—by which he means opposition to war, which is directed against the *symptom,* not against its *cause,* which is the want of principle among the nations. " Reform " is only " changing externals leaving the reality untouched." Fried calls his own system " Revolutionary Pacifism." The word " Revolutionary " he does not use in a political sense. He does not mean the use of violent means for bringing in the new order, but the development of the moral sense, the change of aim, the renewal of purpose, the change of principle. Fried later on alters the word

" Revolutionary " to " causal " (ursachlich), and to-day
it is classically scientific.   It is not concerned so much
with war as with the state of anarchy between nations.
Of what use is it, it asks, if Reform Pacifism, or a universal vague, misty, humanitarian love of Peace endeavours
to evade war, or if war does break out, to humanise it
and lessen its horrors ?   He who wishes to make an
end of war must have something constructive to replace
it.   Therefore, at the Hague Conference of 1899, the
classic Pacifists were the strongest opponents of disarmament unless it included an organisation for the
administration of international justice.   Causal Pacifism, in its logical system—entirely free as it is of far-
fetched idealism—does not even place arbitration in
the first line as a prevention of war, and for this reason :
that wars do not really spring from conflicts about
common sense and justice, or from calm difference
of opinion as to the demands of justice, but from deep-
seated irrational individual and national passions which
are clearly against common sense and justice.   This
or that acute cause of strife is perhaps only an excuse,
the fuse which kindles the flame and the barriers set up
by the imposing court of arbitration are destroyed.
Nothing can restrain it, neither arbitration nor disarmament can curb the war-lust of the individual
groups—nothing will do that till the tension of feeling is
relieved, and how is that to be accomplished ?   The
last word has not been spoken on this point, but we
have the conception given us by keen constructive
Pacifism, and that is : A supernational organisation of
States. Conflicts arise from the want of a sense of
unity and from the fact that this unity is made terribly
difficult for nations or individuals through the defensive
political attitude of the nations to-day.   If that were
removed nothing unnatural would happen, but on the
contrary something of the greatest importance to human

nature and necessary for its development. For man is, as *zoon politikon* dependent on his neighbour and the closer, organically and mechanically, through ties of blood, through intercourse or culture, by biology or civilisation, he comes to his brother in other lands, the closer he must come to him politically. If political confederation is accomplished then, anyway, *extra*-political conflicts will cease. We have examples of this truth in the confederation of small States. War is overcome amongst them, whereas previously it easily broke out. If we look beyond the abnormal difficulties of the moment, we realise that war between North and South Germany is unthinkable. Rather more than half a century ago such a war took place. Community of interests has made it impossible. Could not such an alliance take far larger dimensions so that all nations should be closely knit together in one great confedera-tion ? Of course such a confederation would be much more difficult than between small States of the same race and speaking the same language, but after all, all men are brothers and their interests could so combine that the political union would only be the natural outcome of their own felt need. At the Peace Congress of Paris, in 1849, Victor Hugo said : " If four hundred years ago anyone had told the people of Lorraine, Picardy, Normandy, Brittany, that the day would come when they would no longer fight with arms and cannon, but in their place would be a box for votes, all serious and sensible people, and all great politicians would have said : ' Oh, dreamers ! How little do you know mankind ! What nonsense ! What absurdity ! ' But time has passed and this dream, this folly, has come true."

Pacifism, seeing what culture and scientific develop-ment have already done, believes that the work of political confederacy will go further, and endeavours to hasten it without disregarding the laws of organic growth, not because men are wiser and better, but because the logic of facts and the mechanism of national interests—and perhaps also law immanent in the world—are stronger than the evil will of mankind. Herein lies the path of development which points to a possibility, if not to a necessity. Domestic and scientific internationalism stand on a firmer footing to-day, in spite of the severe setback of the World War. It would not put up with a continuous political and warlike unrest, and certainly will not allow it to continue indefinitely. For politics and war must eventually submit to the interests of the strongest in each particular country. In war individual interests become the interests of the State : for example, the State cannot feed the people without the help of the great firms and ship-owners ; nor can the State be independent of the support of many other influential groups, and these groups are becoming more and more a universal society.

The organisations of these world-societies look on causal Pacifism as their primary task. It alone can furnish a sure basis for arbitration. Till the countries are united to each other by common duties and acknowledge a common sovereign authority, no arbitration will suffice. For it to be able to function, the various countries must be united by some kind of alliance.

Naturally Pacifism desires that a court of arbitration should attempt its utmost even before this supreme alliance of States and nations can be affected, and in the course of history attempts have been made more or less successfully. There exists a list of wars that have been averted. The bloody conflicts of the nations leave their traces in the book of history. Posterity does not hear of those that have been averted, and the pen of the historian slips lightly over them though they are truly history-making facts. Fried, in his "*Handbook*," numbers between 1904 and 1910 seventeen cases which represented a *casus belli*, and which, in earlier days, would certainly have resulted in war, but which were settled peacefully through conferences. We shall take one instance. In the night of October 21st, 1904, the Russian Baltic Fleet, on its way to the Far East, bombarded, on the Doggerbank, fifty English fishing boats from Hull, causing loss of life and destruction of property. There was great indignation in England, and, as Russia was much weakened by the Japanese war, the moment would have been very favourable for England to have declared hostilities. Warlike preparations were begun in Portsmouth Dockyard ; but on October 28th, Russia's proposal of an international court of enquiry was accepted. This court met in Paris on February 9th, 1905, and by February 25th the matter was peacefully settled.

Quite lately, in the Autumn of 1923, the very serious dispute between Italy and Greece, caused by the murder of an Italian Consul, was also decided by an Ambassadors' Court of Arbitration. These courts bring the nations ever nearer together, and pave the way for an organised alliance. Only after further development shall we arrive at one or more supernational tribunals of justice which will be able to fulfil their object.

What would happen if a State belonging to this world organisation were to refuse to submit to its ruling ? This certainly could not happen often, for the interest involved in keeping peaceful relationships with the other allied States would be too great ; but if it did happen, then this League of Nations could employ very strong measures in the interests of Peace, such as boycotting merchandise, obstruction of railway and postal services and international credit. Only when all such measures have failed can force be employed. For such cases an international army would be necessary which could be used against the recalcitrant State.

The discussion on this point in " *Friedenswarte* " (a magazine called Expectations of Peace) in 1923 is most interesting. A German politician, Hellmuth von Gerlach, and four soldiers, the French General Sarrail, the German Major F. C. Enches and Generals von Schönaich and von Daimling, discussed the question of one common army for the nations in an alliance. They not only fully concur in the main, but they even went into several technical and military details, and suggested how the idea could be carried out even in the present imperfect condition of the League of Nations. The two Generals, von Schönaich and von Daimling, do not consider the maintenance of an international army necessary. In their opinion the Police Force of every country under the command of the League of Nations would suffice. However the question is to be answered, it is remarkable that soldiers in high positions consider the disbanding of standing armies possible, and that they look forward to the full development of the idea of the League of Nations. "Everlasting Peace" will not, in the opinion of these Pacifists, prevail completely in the future organisation of the nations, but war in the sense it has hitherto borne will cease. The failure of the administration of supernational Justice might conceivably cause certain nations to appeal to arms instead of to the Courts of Justice. The tribunal of the nations would mobilise the army of the alliance, but only in the cause of justice. They would only be fighting against internal revolt, a strong and just Police action. An external war would only be possible against States outside the alliance, for instance, uncivilised colonies. The aim, of course, of the League of

Nations is that all should belong to it, in which case external war would also cease.

How, then, does causal or organised Pacifism seek to accomplish this great work of the future?

The work to be done includes restoring, increasing, and deepening international relationships through private and public meetings, especially the yearly congress for promoting the world's Peace, begun in 1889, inter-Parliamentary Conferences under the auspices of existing Pacifist organisations, and propaganda through meetings and pamphlets. The intentions of the friends of Peace are thus given wide publicity. It must be acknowledged that already in certain thorny extra-political situations, Pacifist organisations have intervened and have worked successfully for a peaceful solution. By these means there has been opportunity for truly patriotic work.

(b) RELIGIOUS PACIFISM

The Pacifism we have described is classic in its cause and in its form, humanitarian in its motives, scientific or causal in its methods. Its object is justice and its course is evolutionary. It is impossible to raise any sensible objection to it. Its realisation may be despaired of, but no one can question its ideal : which is nothing less than the building up of the system of right and justice as opposed to the anarchical system of might. This is undeniable excepting to an enemy of justice and humanity.

This Pacifism can, however, be criticised on its negative side as to what it does *not* express. It fails on two points—insight into the terrible upset of human nature which is at the root of all conflicts between nations, and on the other side a too feeble opposition in its activities to the power of its opponents, militarism and nationalism. An excessive optimism results from these two mistakes, which takes the accomplishment of the Pacifist aim too easily and the necessary work too lightly. Fried allows quite cheerfully that the result of Pacifism will not be to do away entirely with the spirit of opposition amongst the nations, and adds " that indeed is not necessary—we do not want to turn the nations into angels. Pacifism does not preach brotherhood and the rule of Love. All it preaches is common sense." In these words he acknowledges a want of what Fr. W. Foerster calls " a tragic outlook on life, a strong sense of the power of original sin, a true estimate of the inconceivable weakness of most men." Of course it is possible for what Kant calls " the mechanism of nature " to bring about the political development of the world-wide organisations, but if this mechanical world-wide organisation has no higher strength, if the technical building, however great, has no ethical or religious foundation, then after all not much has been gained. Can the building stand on only " mechanical" supports ? Will it not be another Tower of Babel, if it rests only on human wit and human strength ? Will it not collapse in the day of trial in a whirlwind of confusion ?

This is the objection raised by the religious party against the Pacifism of pure reason and common sense. Common sense and mechanism are not enough for the restoration and maintenance of the world's peace, and we want something deeper, built on Ethics and Religion. From this comes *religious* Pacifism, which is distinguished from the purely humanitarian Pacifism by the motives upon which it bases the obligation to labour for Peace. It is for the sake of God and His Kingdom, or, if we express this subjectively, for the sake of Conscience, Justice and Love that we strive. At last the friends of Peace are beginning to use simpler, more spontaneous, more thorough means. To-day Pacifists, whether from the humanitarian or religious point of view, are coming together.

Long after the early centuries of the Christian era, when the Church had shown her disapproval of war by treating those who had shared in it as sinners requiring cleansing, the Quakers originated an opposition to war, grounded on Religion. As this movement has endured till the present time in all its strength, it is necessary for us to examine it. Quakerism is a very good example of what we have already considered, i.e. that these Christian Sects lay hold of one Truth with tremendous fervour and push all the other equally important truths into the background. The Quakers are as impressed with the command of Christ to love one another as were the early Christians. They are as devoted in their works of mercy, which are unsurpassed by any denomination. In the seventeenth century George Fox founded a community of religious enthusiasts who depended entirely on the " Inner light " and refused any human authority or revelation, even Holy Scripture itself. Fox had interrupted the preacher in an English Cathedral with the cry : " It is not scripture, it is the spirit by whom the Holy Prophets wrote and spoke." He meant to say : The letter profiteth nothing, even the letter of Holy Scripture, it is the spirit of inward Grace and illumination and strength which comes from God and by which man becomes a living Christ. A great truth, but one which should not eliminate the objective and all-embracing character of the Bible. This the Quakers did and do to this day. They evade all dogmatic and symbolic Christianity, they have neither creed nor sacrament, not even Baptism, nor Liturgy.

All Christ's stinging words about the necessity of the Faith, the Church and the Church's authority are replaced by the witness they believe they have within—

K

of the spirit of God. They only acknowledge as binding the social and ethical commands of Christ, and these they try to fulfil with no compromise and with much self-sacrifice. The " Church Christians " accuse the Quakers of being too much " on the other side," that they look on this world as only a vale of woe and that it is no use trying to improve it. Therefore slavery, war and other ills just have to go on. We shall return to this reproach later on.

To the Quaker who would practise the simple ethics of Love taught by our Lord, the condemnation of war is inevitable. There is no room for discussion—it is simply the spirit of Christ. The world, the State, material interests, may say what they like, Christ forbids all hatred, revenge, envy and has commanded all men to love even their enemies, to do them good and to overcome evil only with good. No one possessed by this spirit can kill his brother, or wound him ; therefore war is impossible. The power of the State is limited by the word of God and by conscience and both tell us that God must be obeyed before man. The good of the State, too, is never really furthered by war. We are the true patriots who maintain that he who takes the sword, who puts his trust in blood and iron, shall perish by the sword, that is, by blood and iron, even though it may not be for a long time. The Quakers, through refusing military service, have conflicted sharply with the State. That they know and wish. We find in one of their manifestos that " they believe the Kingdom of God can only come when a group of men will be found who have already, in this difficult world of to-day, ' put its laws into practice, whose Faith is strong enough to dare to live according to them and even to die for them. Lastly they are convinced that the Truth and devotion of Christ, which cost Him His Life, have made this path a Holy duty for men. The Quaker is convinced that the possibility of a true, free, perfect kingdom in the future depends, to some extent, on his present conduct. He acts in the name of the unborn community for whose Holy Rights he is responsible."

In the course of history, hundreds of Quakers in this frame of mind have been imprisoned. In the last war they were divided, some serving as stretcher bearers and nurses, etc.—others refusing to support war even indirectly. The latter were imprisoned. Many who were not eligible for active service and, therefore, not imprisoned, did good work in the devastated regions of France ; others did what they could to alleviate the misery and starvation of Russia.

Quakers support all organised work for Peace, but that is not enough, for they find that religious inspiration is wanting. In a manifesto to the Christian Churches in all lands they say : " We are convinced that this object (the maintenance of Peace) can only be accomplished through refusing to take any share in war, for the simple reason that war is a direct contradiction of the message and spirit of the life and death of Christ. The idea of Peace, which comes from the depths of Christianity, involves a firm refusal to fight, without any compromise. On these terms the position of the Christian Church is quite clear : neither persuasion nor force can compel her to share in any preparation for war or to give it any Christian Blessing."

The awakening of deep religious conviction always precedes in history any great moral change. Strength has never been wanting, amongst really earnest-minded men inspired by a living and decided Christianity, and by them the Kingdom of God on earth is advanced step by step. " What greater message of joy and restoration for mankind could be given us to-day than the assurance that all who bear the name of Christ in all countries are determined to take no part in war or in its preparations, but in future are united to labour for Peace by peaceful methods only ?   Should one not profess this venture of faith in true fellowship, and in that spirit of love which bears all things and believes and hopes all things, and overcomes all things, and is never put to shame ?   Shall the torch of spiritual heroism be borne aloft by the Church of the Living Christ, or shall the leadership in this desperate struggle against war fall from our hands and be taken up by others whose souls are braver and truer ? "

The Quakers are the most important of the religious Pacifists.   Count Leo Tolstoi and his small following are one with them in opposition to war on religious grounds, but otherwise he differs from them radically.

Tolstoi was an extreme radical, a reversed Nietzsche, and in practical significance his teachings must be taken even less seriously than Nietzsche's.   Tolstoi's absolute anarchism which denies all authority, all order and organisation, is condemned already, in spite of occasional beautiful and inspiring thoughts, to remain only empty words.   When the poet turns to drama, as in the play, " Light shining in darkness," his ideas may be useful in exciting feeling against social evils.   His philosophical writings, however, are so opposed to common sense and natural feeling that it would be waste of time to consider them.   His influence in one direction has been completely opposed to Quakerism, and where are any positive results of his message of Peace compared to what the Quakers have done ?   The Quaker, Corder Catchpool, in his report of their campaign against war, in the modest and yet decided manner of his co-religionists, concludes with the words : " This was, on the whole, a passive Peace campaign.   The Friends know that Peace is something active—a life that is to be led, and now that the war is over the time for its testing and its real usefulness has come."

Among Protestant Religious communities are two international organisations that may be counted as religious Pacifists : *The world alliance for the friendly work of the Church* and *the " Alliance of Reconciliation "* (Versöhnungsbund). The Secretary of State of the world alliance, Theophilus Mann, tells us how his Society arose. " In the beginning of the century, Europe, armed to the teeth, seemed even to herself to be something unnatural, and so the Hague Peace Conference came about, but of course they were a branch of the governments of the various States, and were arranged by diplomats and lawyers. The Churches had no say in them. Certain Christian men and women asked themselves whether one of the first duties of the Christian Churches was not the endeavour to promote good and friendly relationships between the nations ? The answer was ' yes '—and this meant getting to work. In a short time they had messages of co-operation from all over the world. A deputation was sent to the Hague, and a Memorial drawn up in English, French, and German, speaking of the desire and the obligation of Christians to co-operate in the work for Peace. This memorial was solemnly presented to the President of the Peace Conference."

The world alliance (Weltbund) was founded in August, 1914. Its immediate object was the common interests of the various Protestant Churches, but an important aim is " the bridging over, or better still, the overcoming of the international and social separation of mankind." The *versöhnungsbund* does its work independently of any Church organisation in opposition to international capitalism. " The basis of our work," we are told in their statutes, " is the conviction that all men, as Christ tells us, are brothers who should help and serve one another. The object of our alliance is by combating unjust class distinctions—world-wide or domestic—to reconcile all men of all classes and all nations without distinction of race or religion."

The editor of the Catholic Monthly Magazine, " The care of souls " (*die Seelsorge*), Prof. H. Hoffman, on the invitation of the founder and leader of the Alliance of Reconciliation, assisted at its inauguration at Nyborg, on the Island of Fünen, in June, 1923, and made a most favourable impression. The meeting was deeply religious. Each session began and ended with prayer. The atmosphere was charged with Christian love. All were kindled with one desire, to hasten the advent of the Kingdom of God, in order that justice and love should guide men's dealings with one another. This spirit of Peace was displayed in the mutual intercourse which was marked by most considerate mutual love. It is a well-known fact that there are very many Pacifist Jews. The reason is that they are less firmly rooted than other races in the political nationalities of to-day. Also they are more disposed to internationalism through their history, their intelligence and their occupations. Richard Nicolas Coudenhove-Kalergi gives an interesting reason for this phenomenon : " The people who have suffered the most from injustice are called to free the world from injustice ; the people who have suffered the most from the rule of might are called to free the world from that rule." " As a civilised people the Jews are centuries older than the Germanic races of Europe—here lies the root of their Pacifism. As in individual life, the young love fighting more than the old, so also the older civilisations are more pacifist."

(c) YOUNG PACIFISM

Neither classic Pacifism, which takes no account of Religion, nor the religious Friends of Peace, for whom scientific and organised Pacifism does not go deep enough, are primarily concerned with an international, organised kingdom of this world.

The most advanced among them, without giving up their co-operation in the political organisation of the future, are in direct conflict with recognised national precepts as to war, and decline, whatever the consequences, to have any part or lot in it.

There are other Pacifists however, whose methods are different from those of the Pacifists of the old school, because that older way is not quick or sure enough.

They are so far one with classic Pacifism in holding that the international system of *might* must be replaced by an international system of *right*.

But how long will it take for the world to get so far ?

What use is it if we and our children, in spite of all the surrounding culture, are to be sacrificed to the Moloch of war ? What became of Pacifism in 1914 ?

Was it not bankrupt in spite, or perhaps because, of its classic theories and its quiet ? To this Pfarrer Umfrid, a representative of the old school, very truly answers " How can a dying man dare to abuse the doctor whose orders he has never obeyed." The outbreak of the World War was, after all, only a proof of what a misfortune the isolation of States, the want of international understanding, the domineering influence of militarism was, to the existing, but half asleep and inadequately-organised, spirit of Peace in the masses of the population of all countries.

The older Pacifists also say that the war itself is a striking example of the justice and necessity of their ideas. Very well, say the young ones, we shall work with you, but you do not go quick enough, and on one point you have been proved wrong : your theory of the justification of a war of defence (as opposed to offence) has been tested *ad absurdum,* for none of the powers wanted anything but a defensive war. They all told their subjects that the existence of their Fatherland was at stake and must be defended against immediate danger. So it will always be !

There is only one way that will help for the moment : radical opposition to war, in any shape, by calling a general strike and appealing to the masses to refuse military service.

Even during this war, this radical Pacifism showed itself—mostly in England and America. Most of the supporters were Quakers, but many were of quite other persuasions. As England had an alternative service, either military or various forms of auxiliary service, a good many were able to quiet their conscience by joining the Army Service Corps.

The others were imprisoned in concentration camps.

After the war a movement arose in England, and also in France and Germany, under the name of the " No More War Movement." Its supporters protested every year on July 29th (the anniversary of the outbreak of war) in hundred of towns by means of mass meetings, and made the following declaration :

" Believing that all war is unjust and that the arming of the nations on land, on sea, and in the air, is a betrayal of the spiritual unity and mutual understanding of the human race, I declare my intention never to take part in any war, either offensive or defensive, either through service or production or sale of munitions, nor will I, of my free will, take up any war loan, nor by my work set others free to join up. I further declare my intention to work for the removal of causes of war and to strive for a new social order which rests on common endeavour for the common good."

As the English name, " conscientious objectors," implies, they justify their opposition to war by appealing to the voice of conscience. We have not the right to question their honesty, but it is a fact that strong political and purely selfish grounds account for much of the objecting. In England and America the Anglo-Saxon spirit of liberty rebelled against conscription. If a man wishes to be a soldier, let him. If he does not, he is not to be compelled.

This was the opinion of many Anglo-Saxons who had no sympathy with the objectors.

Others suspected that the objectors were only shirking their duty to give even their life for their country.

Of course, we do not find this motive acknowledged, but it is impossible not to feel that it accounted for much of the Young Pacifism.

Dr. Kurt Hiller, a pioneer of their theories, declares : " We, the young generation, maintain as the first of all subjective Rights in the State, the Right of each individual to dispose of his own life. Our existence on this wonderful planet is too short and too beautiful for us to give any earthly power that Right which, from the beginning, has belonged only to the unsearchable. The sacredness of human life—alas not as reality and fact—but still as idea and what we look forward to—is the basis of our critical and political thoughts and therefore our Pacifism. We shall neither be killed nor kill. We therefore scorn military service (which is really compulsion to kill and be killed), and we make no distinction between defensive or offensive wars."

Naturally these arguments prevail most where another world is not believed in.

Those who do not believe in life after death must always feel that taking of life is the greatest of all ills.

We feel the tragic passion with which those cling to life in whose name Dr. Helene Stöcker writes : " They have learnt with Nietzsche to prize life above all things, all the more because believing what they do about this world, they can have no hope of a hereafter where they would be rewarded. I consider it a sign of man's increasing self-respect that the value of the individual, the personal, can never again be disregarded and that he therefore insists that this precious, one and only, and irreplaceable life should be protected from insensate disturbance. We are on the highest step of organic life—as it is known to us—truly the Lords and Creators of all things, and we are to fulfil our highest development—in complete self-consciousness."

Certainly the Faithful are not to belittle human life, taught, as they are, by the fifth commandment to respect both their life and that of others. Christ ratified this command when he went to the cause of all destruction of life and condemned passion and hatred and slander. But Christ teaches the joyful sacrifice of life in the service of the higher good : obedience, justice and again, love—not of self, but of others. " Greater love hath no man than this, that a man lay down his life for his friends." These words may be true of war, truer still of the warrior, especially if he risks his life in obedience to the command of superiors put over him by God and from love to his neighbours, his fellow-countrymen, without hating his enemies, in defence of the unjustly attacked and where there is no other possible means of restoring moral justice. For these reasons classic Pacifism has, till now, never condemned a defensive war, even if thousands of lives were lost. It is truly a sacrifice for friends. " Life is not the greatest good, but guilt is the greatest evil," and cowardice and idle endurance are very real guilt.

If one country is attacked without provocation by another, the life and property of its inhabitants destroyed, it would only be meeting one sin with another if the attacked country did not defend itself to the uttermost.

This is the undoubted theory of the older Pacifists, from which they have never swerved. One of the worthiest of them, Walter Schücking, states his point : " In certain circumstances, it seems to me, he stands higher who, against his inclination, defends his neighbours by his arms, than he who tamely submits to injustice. I can only understand the moral greatness of our Lord's teaching that we are not to withstand evil, as meaning that I, personally, must bear evil done me, but it equally lays upon us the duty to defend my fellow countrymen from wrong."

This theory of defensive war cannot be criticised. In practice it is unfortunately only a sad caricature.

The case of one country attacking another for sheer lust of blood or conquest is unlikely under modern conditions. There is always some question of Rights. Almost always a bloodless solution would be possible, and it is practically out of the question in these days that even a defensive war would " further good and avoid evil " and be restricted within the limits of Justice and Love—that is that the third and fourth conditions required by the moral law to justify war would be present. Thus the word " defensive " comes to be misused.

Partly from the criticism both of Religion, Pacifism and Young Pacifism, but chiefly from devastating experience, grave doubts have arisen in the circles of classic Pacifism as to the justification even of defensive war. Such a firm supporter of the rights of nations, as Hans Wehberg, allows that what may be justifiable theoretically, may be wrong when put into practice, and he lays stress on the doubtful results of defensive wars : so that we see even classic Pacifism reconsidering its principles.

What is necessary at present is not to destroy belief in the justification of defensive war in itself, but in its use as a means for the preservation of moral order. Catholic moral theology teaches that in national law " moral " has the same meaning as " according to reason," that answering to the Reason of God and its reflection in the spirit and conscience of man. War, therefore, which is not according to reason, and contradicts its object, which is the restitution of justice, is immoral. This may even be said of a defensive war, if it oversteps the " *moderamen inculpatae tutelae* " (the measure of justifiable protection), if, even though it is defensive, more harm than good will come, if it will cause great suffering to the whole civilised world, if, in a word, it will increase the evil it is out to cure.

In these circumstances even a defensive war is not " reasonable " and, therefore, is not morally permissible; but, we ask, is an invasion to be meekly submitted to ? Certainly not.

The moral ordering of the world requires some sort of defence.

The development of the Law of Nations has already made such progress that international protection is guaranteed to the attacked State. The Geneva Peace Protocol, signed in the autumn of 1924 by the representatives of fifty-five States, declares an offensive war to be " an international crime " and decrees common means of coercion against the attacking State. The attacked State is bound to take steps in self-defence which means to go to war. We still ask is there no other solution, and we consider another means which is supported by strong moral reasons, i.e. well-organised, passive resistance.

One of the first striking examples of the power of this weapon was the suppression of the Kapp-Putches in Germany, in March, 1920. It was a military attack on the new German Government. In a few hours the military party had seized the reins of Government ;

but in those days the attempt had failed. Why? As a result of armed opposition? In the districts where the Putsch was resisted by force the struggle lasted for weeks; but where the rising was met by passive resistance, it went out in smoke. Mars is weaker than Mercury.

Work and Home are stronger than the " mailed fist."

If new Germany had fought old Germany, the whole country would have been torn to pieces.

The passions of war spring from hot blood which naturally seeks an outlet in fighting—it is instinctive. Passive resistance, on the contrary, comes from the mind—no hot, boisterous blood—at its best it is the Spirit of Jesus Christ and bears His Message.

Then reason tells us that spiritual powers, working themselves out in the great undertakings and organisations of modern States, must, in the long run, prevail over brute force. Of course " the mailed fist " and poison gas can destroy the finest products of civilisation and lay waste whole countries, but eventually such destruction would fail against a country that declined to appeal to arms.

The most important point is : How about Honour? Does not defencelessness mean loss of Honour?

Everyone allows that a modern war, however justifiable, injures a country most terribly, even if it does not destroy it ; but loss or gain is not the point when it is a question of honour or dishonour. Often the best people cling to a defensive policy because they believe it preserves material, if not ideal, well-being. Now Pacifism will fail if it has no satisfactory solution to offer. But it can meet the difficulty, for what the sense of honour rightly lays stress on is the weakness, the want of energy, the shrinking from sacrifice, the meek submitting to injustice. Does passive resistance, however, necessarily involve this weakness ? We are told that such a defensive is far harder than any military defensive, for the attacker and potential victor will certainly not submit meekly to his command being defied.

Military occupation of a civilised country would also be banned. If authority were resisted by the accredited means adopted by Pacifists, namely boycotting and strikes, which would then be justifiable and indeed obligatory, the result would be imprisonment, shortage of food, even execution.

The Pacifist argues that, if nations were educated to make these sacrifices, as they are now educated to regard war, if this doctrine were taught in Church and school, and were held by the best and most high-minded of the population, there would be no more talk of the cowardice and weakness and want of honour of Pacifism. That the victory would be with the children of Light, not with the armies of Darkness—victory as assured as that of the young Christianity against the old power of Paganism, when the Imperialism of Rome broke in pieces, not before the sword, but before the Cross— before the power of passive resistance—moral goodness winning over material strength. If all this were realised Pacifism has no doubt that defensive war as the only means of protection against attack or restitution of justice would become absurd, as would the idea that vindication of honour demanded bloodshed.

(2) WITHIN THE CHURCH

The Catholic Church has always been reproached for two reasons. Either she concerns herself too much with the things of this world, or she does not concern herself enough.

If she interferes in national or social quarrels she is said to have forgotten her purely religious mission. If she does not interfere, she has lost her mission as spiritual and moral leader of civilisation.

She no longer has the courage and strength to keep the temporal powers in their places and to lay her veto on the sins of the mighty as she had in her best days. Thus she is either too national and partial, or too international and impartial. We see this especially in the great political developments of the world. Some say the Church must refrain from any interference, others that she should take her place even to the extent of excommunicating. Whatever she does is wrong.

Even her own children do not refrain from criticism. Of course the Church is not misled by this cross-fire. Still the clamour of tongues shows how difficult it is to reach the happy medium. Affairs of State do, on principle, come within the competency of the Church as far as they concern the moral life, but things become so complicated, under modern conditions, that it is extremely difficult to draw the line.

We can easily realise how difficult it is for the Church, especially for the Holy See, to give any guidance in matters of dispute between States that is certain to be right, when the questions are so involved and right and wrong seem to shift almost from hour to hour.

Those who think that the Popes have been too passive on questions of Peace and war, theoretical and practical, in the last hundred years, may take this to heart—that the Papacy has not taken a prominent part in the Peace movements of the day because the Church herself is the great Peacemaker, the universal Power of Unity and Peace whose voice, if it were listened to, would bring Peace and political unity.

But, whatever may have been the attitude of Catholics and their leaders, in the past, to Peace movements, the Great War which shook the world to its foundations, certainly moved the Church most deeply, and one

Pope was found who adopted the Programme of Classic Pacifism and called forth a new and strong movement in the Church in that direction.

Benedict XV.'s predecessors had opposed war and given their sympathy to organised Pacifism. At the beginning of the Crimean War, Pius IX. said : " War must cease and be driven off the earth." The same Pope wrote to King Wilhelm I. of Prussia at the outbreak of the Franco-Prussian war on July 22nd, 1870 : " Our most earnest wish is to live to see wars and disputes at an end and the terrible sufferings involved prevented."

Leo XIII., who was distinguished by his clear vision of the shadows of the present and the dangers of the future, as Bishop of Perugia in his Pastoral of 1878, exposed pitilessly the Macchiavellian precept of the triumph of might over right, of greed over justice ; and as Pope he drew the attention of Catholics to the mania for armament of the European States—the " armed Peace " against which Pacifism had always protested.

In his allocution of February, 1889, he speaks of the " ever-increasing disinclination of the nations to war," and he wrote to the first international Peace Congress, in Paris, in 1889, these noble and encouraging words : " Nothing is so important as to divert the danger of war from Europe, therefore every endeavour in that direction must be looked upon as a step in the right direction."

In 1894 he says, in the Encyclical *Praeclara* : " Youths are taken away from the care and teaching of their parents and cast into the dangers of barrack life. They are taken from the land, from their studies or their business for military service." And he concludes with a reference to the well-nigh unbearable " armed Peace." Leo's successor, Pius X., encouraged the international congress of workers for Peace with the words : " All endeavours for Peace are in harmony with the spirit and precepts of the Gospel."

Just as the Apostolic Epistles were suited to the circumstances of the day, so are the Papal admonitions.

For the last century wars were on a limited scale— the whole of civilisation had not shared in them. There- fore the Holy See had not felt obliged to protest in any special way. But when the " armed Peace " exploded in the Great War, then the watcher on the chair of Peter, Benedict XV., arose and broke out like Jeremias and Isaias in lamentation and sorrow. As early as September 8th, 1914, he appealed to the powers for an armistice. On November 1st, of the same year, he pointed to " other means and ways for adjusting injured rights " and, as the war raged on, he called it " a terrible butchery," "a disgrace to Europe," " a horrible human slaughter," " anti-Christian slaughter."

Such have been the lamentations of the Pope, but he was not merely negative. It was Benedict's unceasing aim to stop the war and heal its wounds ; but when it was at last at an end he pointed out, quite on the lines of Classic Pacifism, how a true and lasting Peace was to be obtained. Benedict's greatest legacy to posterity, besides his living example as a true follower of Christ, is his Encyclical " *Pacem Dei*," of May 23rd, 1920. It begins with the words of St. Augustine that Peace is God's greatest gift to the world, but that the present lull does not deserve the name of Peace. True Peace rests in freedom from hate and enmity, as Christendom has always known. Then the Pope lays stress on love and Peace being the very essence of Christianity. Love and unity are the Marks of Christ. Love of enemies, love and forgiveness for every injury are the condition of the everlasting love—Hatred is murder : " He who hateth his brother is a murderer." The Pope himself has been much criticised, but he forgives his opponents

L

and " embraces them all with love and goodwill." This is the Christian mentality.

As the Saviour went about doing good so must the Christian, and to-day more than ever. Humanity has been robbed by the war and left wounded and ashamed in the road.

Dare the Church pass by on the other side ? Her Faithful must apply themselves zealously to works of mercy. Their leaders of the Priesthood should, the Pope tells us, " be eager for that which constitutes a true grasp of the Christian life, the love of our neighbour, even our enemy." And they must go to the root of the evil and contend against enmity and hatred. Literature and the Press should be used for pity and goodness, and should refrain from hard words, and what applies to individuals must spread to the nations. The Pope proclaims clearly and unhesitatingly that there is only one and the same morality for states and individuals.

He then speaks of the idea of a League of Nations. Now that the war is over, a great union of the nations will develop, rooted not only in Christian love, but as a result of the necessities of the circumstances. They will be drawn to it from necessity as well as from goodwill in consequence of the growth of civilisation : especially the extraordinary increased means of intercommunication. It is much to be wished that all States should lay aside all suspicion and unite together in a great society, or rather, family. The need of such a League of Nations as a check on military ambition which can no longer be supported by the various countries, if for no other reasons, is universally acknowledged. By this means such a murderous and terrible war will be prevented in the future, and each nation within the just limits of its independence will be sure of its own possessions. If once this League of Nations is founded on Christian laws, the demands of justice and love will be met, and certainly the Church will not stand aside. We know from history how feuds and disputes gradually ceased as the old barbarous nations of Europe imbibed the spirit of the Church : by degrees the nations were welded together into one Society and Christian Europe was revealed under the guidance and protection of the Church, the guardian of greatness and well-being, while each nation maintained its independence. The Pope ends the Encyclical as he began it : " that all should be one in that Christian Love which knows no strangers nor foreigners. We further admonish the nations most earnestly, influenced by the Spirit of Christ to determine to establish Peace and to unite together, protected by an enduring Spirit of Justice."

Benedict XV. was a convinced Pacifist. If we put together all the Pope's pronouncements on the subject we have the complete Programme of Classic Pacifism, with the addition of the Christian Ethics of mutual help and the organisation of the universal Church, by which alone the internal health and the external status of the political universal organisation can be assured.

What made the Pope a convinced Pacifist, besides, of course, his knowledge of the Gospel of Christ, was his belief in the practicability of the Pacifist aims. He did not belong to those self-satisfied, " practical Politicians " (real-politikern) who do not believe in the possibility of political improvement. The common phrase, " war has always been," is not in his vocabulary.

Materially war will never cease if men will never give up what Bishop Emmanuel von Ketteler calls " the nation's right of Fist," by which he means the state of anarchy existing between nations. He who does not exalt the policy of *laissez faire* and compromise has to work against this evil right of the Fist—right of might— and a moral force like the Catholic Church is directly called to do so.

Secondly, Benedict acknowledges the essence of Pacifism, which is that the international system of *Might* should be replaced by an international system of *Right*. The Pope says that the first and most important point must be " the substitution of the moral Power of Right for the material Power of Arms. From this follows the possibility of disarmament. The two go side by side." There must be a legal understanding as to reciprocal disarmament, regulated and guaranteed competent to maintain order in the various States.

Benedict also appeals for an international tribunal of Justice possessing authority to enforce its decisions : " Then instead of armies we should have arbitration with its peace-making activities, dealing firmly and without bias with those international questions which would be submitted to it."

The Pope also raised once more the question of the freedom of the sea.

Benedict XV.'s voice was not listened to with much appreciation. To most his was a hard saying, and who could hear it ? Still he had a following. The German Peace Association sent him, twice, a message of thanks, as did various other German Peace Societies. The Turks erected a memorial to him.

In many respects the Pope's views coincided with what were thought to be the views of President Wilson, which did meet with much success.

After four years of hideous war, a real Peace was as impossible for Europe as complete and immediate recovery would be for a sick person who had undergone a severe operation.

The German Priest, Dr. Max Josef Metzger, who had been a war chaplain, responded to the Pope's injunctions and started, in 1916, the White Cross Society, whose members are to work as Catholics for universal Peace. He received the Holy Father's approval and blessing which made his position assured. The headquarters of the White Cross is in Graz, but branches have been established all over Germany.

In France Marc Sangnier led the movement. He had united with the " Société Gratry," a Peace association, in 1907. In those days, however, Sangnier's chief interests were in social matters. His magazine, *Le Sillon*, had great influence, but was condemned by Pius X. Sangnier was allowed to continue his Christian-Democratic work and his daily paper, *La Démocratie*, was approved by the Holy Father. Sangnier was a perfectly loyal son of the Church. Then came the war. Sangnier was First Lieutenant in the Front Line, and in six months he was a Captain. He looked beyond the immediate issue, told his soldiers, in November, 1918, " Our war has not only to do with Germany— No, it is war against war. By untold sacrifice we may claim the right to demand that a new world should arise from the ashes of the old. Away with secret diplomacy, away with those armaments which suck the strength of the nations, away with it all and let brotherly love take its place ; let us have courts of justice instead of brute force, let justice be dealt out to the weak even as to the strong. Now is the accepted time—the opportunity. The wound is open, mankind has undergone a devastating surgical operation. Will any one dare to sew the open wound up without cleansing it from all its horror and corruption ? "

After the war Marc Sangnier went, in the service of national reconciliation, to Poland, Austria, Italy, Belgium and got into communication with leading politicians in Genoa, Rome, Vienna and Berlin. He was, therefore, able to convene the first democratic Peace Congress in Paris, which was attended by delegates from twenty-one countries. Benedict XV. sent his Blessing, the Papal Nuncio, Mgr. Cerretti, invited the members

of the Congress to his Palace, and at the concluding
meeting Sangnier converted 4,000 members, for the
time at any rate, to his high ideal.

In the next year Sangnier called a Peace Congress
in Vienna. The membership had increased, but the
enthusiasm and results were less than in Paris. The
success of the Third Congress, in Freiburg, August
4th–10th, 1923, was all the more remarkable, for here
a whole town was under the influence of the universal,
of the fact of a new world within the old one.

It was not that the members had increased very
much, nor the fact that at the conclusion 7,000 men,
perfectly disciplined, gathered round the pulpit of the
pioneer of Peace, nor that on this occasion the programme had received ecclesiastical approval.

The presence of youth was the leading feature. A
great company of strong, weather-beaten young men,
from all parts of Germany, met at Freiburg to protest
against the false sentimentality that exalts war. It
was no faked affair, it was simply the expression of
a new mentality. This young mentality will conquer
not through hatred and cursing.

Out of the bloody orgies of the war this spirit has
been born, but side by side with this spirit of youth is
another which clings to the old evil traditions of hatred
and ill-will. Of that we do not speak. Only of that
youth which we find represented at Freiburg.

So far this spirit of youth may have appeared light-
hearted and careless, but it has taken the question of
war and Peace very seriously both on the moral and
intellectual side.

There is, even among the young Germans, a movement towards a brotherly understanding with France.
The breach between the two countries is, as they
recognise, so wide that no natural bridge can span it,
but, as humble followers of Christ, they say we might

try to lay aside hatred, bitterness, mistrust and revenge, and more than that : to render good for evil with the folly of the Cross. Let us go to the devastated provinces of France and there, with our own hands, try to build up what the war has destroyed. It is to be a new and bloodless crusade.

In this frame of mind some go to a priest whose Church has been destroyed, and offer to build it up ; others to Convents, who long to get their schools or orphanages back ; or to a Burgomaster, who wants his schools restored ; or to those who have been crippled by the war ; or to the widows ; so that the fields which have been made like the road to hell may be again the fields of God.

For the moment there has not been much result. The difficulties are great. For instance, it is very difficult to get passports from one country to the other, but that the call has been responded to by hundreds of humble Christians is a proof that the Sermon on the Mount still has undying Power.

Nor is this young growth a children's Crusade : it is strong young men who have dedicated themselves in the prime of their life to this work.

. . . . .

This is not the end of the struggles of our Catholic youth after Purity and Devotion. Many seek to go still further and deeper. They ask not only about this or that war and our responsibility in the concrete, but how about war as a metaphysical and moral fact ? Can it ever be good if it is arraigned at the bar of true justice ? If not why do men to whom we owe honour and respect still trifle with it ? If it can be good where do we find this stated in the Gospels, and what are its limits, and how far may we share in it ?

In " *Pfingst Feuer* "* (Fire of Pentecost), Franz Kloidt puts this before his Catholic readers in an article called *A great question*.   He says : " Fighting between towns or provinces of the same State is impossible to-day, because such a breach of Peace is not war as *ultima ratio*.   Why is it immoral ?   Can it not serve as *ultima ratio* ? "

He concludes : " It is our business to get to the bottom of things, as far as possible.   Here is a fundamental question.   A clear answer to it will not only clear the air in political conflicts and help those who have been beating themselves against these unsolved questions to a clearer outlook.   Not only will our united investigation of questions of national and international politics be a source of light . . . but also division of hearts will almost entirely cease within the Catholic Church.   Who will help us to the Light ? "

In the circles of the young Catholic movement there are too points which are always coming up : Nature and Jesus Christ.   There is in this youth a strong urge back to nature and to a natural manner of life, to happy intercourse with nature, and also back to Christ, Who is above nature, " the Master Who raises and ennobles it."

With the eyes of the child of nature and the child of God this Christian Brotherhood considers these questions about Peace and war.   What do both nature and Christ say as to the murder of fellow-students and fellow-Christians ?   Is it natural ?   Is it Christian ?   The answer rings out clearly : No.   And to the further question : May we share in it ?   Again the answer comes from impatient, uncompromising youth—No.

Whatever we may think of this drastic solution, it is

---

* 2nd year, vol. 2.

here. We have with us this radical young Catholic Pacifism. It speaks by word and by writing from friend to friend, or friend to foe. It has been spread by the monthly magazine, " *Vom frohen Leben* " (Happy Life).

We are shown how modern war in its cause and still more in its results contradicts our moral sense. Modern war with the all-round ruin it brings must be immoral.

Further, we are told that all war is un-Christian, because there must be no limitation. We must be given up absolutely to the Spirit of Christ and to the following of His example without any reserve or mitigations.

It is allowed that there have been righteous wars in the course of history, e.g. the war against Turkey, though if other means had been adopted it would have been more in accordance with the Spirit of Christ. But it is not considered that anything can justify modern warfare and its practices. It is immoral and un-Christian and it follows that military service is to be refused. No authorities have the right to impose it. War is against the Law of God and so the State must not be obeyed if military service is enforced.

These thoughts differ from Quakerism and from the young Pacifism outside the Church. Quakers and other conscientious objectors condemn all war, all armed defence of any kind. The young Catholics distinguish between just and unjust war, though they are not very clear as to where the difference lies. They differ from many non-Catholic young objectors in their motive power. No young man should consider himself superior to his companion, who obeys the call to arms. Yes, he may be very much his inferior for there is a poor, feeble, unmanly Pacifism without any strength or greatness, a compulsory Pacifism from bodily weakness or a sham Pacifism from cowardice. Such are contemptible and it gives one food for thought that one of the young men of the other camp, Max Boudy, says : " I have never yet found a Pacifist whose Pacifism inspired him with such inner beauty as I have found in several men for whom war, under certain circumstances, was a reasonable, justifiable, if tragic, necessity." Such remarks must be taken seriously. They impose inner and outer obligations. If it is not to be a bloodless intellectualism or a weak, cowardly quietism, or a luxurious epicureanism, Pacifism must lay very great stress on bodily discipline, on culture, on bodily and mental development.

More than all, he who opposes war must be inwardly clean. His passion for justice must not be tainted by hidden uncleanness. As long as Pacifists are in the minority let them begin with a steady fight against all that is evil in themselves.

So we see that the Catholic Associations of the young against war are based on religious and moral motives.

The spirit of the Gospel is their moving power and it demands a strong spirit of sacrifice. From the negative side it is the conviction that modern warfare, based, as it is, on hatred, revenge and greed, is criminal with its brutal methods and terrible results. Its formula in moral theology is the doubtfulness of the *causa justa* and the *intentio recta*—that good is furthered and evil hindered—the absence of the *debitus modus*—of the four conditions stipulated by Suarez and Bellarmin for the justification of war, " that it should be conducted within the limits of justice and love."

This conviction as to war has not been learnt by Catholic youth from ecclesiastical lore, or even from books of moral theology. They have learnt it from nature, from their hearts, and from the Sacred Heart itself.

But being convinced that both nature and Christ are opposed to modern warfare they seek with their whole soul for the Church's support for their position. " We hope that war will be overcome through the Church and even if, after two thousand years, this hope is unfulfilled we still hope and go on knocking at the door like the importunate man in the Gospel." This knocking at the door of their Church from love of Peace and love of their fellow men and love of Christ, has something stirring in it. Just as faithful Catholics wait with pious impatience for the definition of a dogma, which has long belonged to the " Faith-consciousness " of the Church, so and more fervently innumerable Catholics are waiting for a moral definition about war, for a decisive word as to its immorality. As good children defend their mother against attacks and misrepresentations, so do they take their Church under their protection when they are asked why she has not done more against war in the past. " What," they ask, " is the history of the Church ? Only to show forth the path of Christ and His Sorrows, Christ and His Spirit in the Church and through the Church to the world, against material-ism, against Satan and the world. In spite of progress, in spite of the short-lived Peace of God in the middle ages, Christ in the Church has not yet been able to take any great steps *against* all war and *towards* general Peace (because men will not consent) ; but now, after the terrible fiasco of war, as Benedict protested in the name of Christ the Prince of Peace, so does Pius stand up protesting against war and, calling for Peace, *Der Sieg des Pazifismus* (the victory of Pacifism), speak out more strongly still."

That the Church should forbid war belongs to those things of which our Lord says : " I have still many things to say unto you but you cannot hear them now." To-day is the time—the fruit is ripe. The condemnation of war is not a contradiction of the Church's history, but its result—its fulfilment.

We see its development from Christ Himself through Augustine and Francis of Assisi till to-day, in the prohibition of military service for Priests, and in the Truce of God of the middle ages. The triumph of Pacifism, the condemnation of war, and the declaration of passive resistance, is just as little opposed to tradition as was the attitude of the Church towards slavery or serfdom, or the dogma of the Immaculate Conception, or the Infallibility of the Pope. Only he who does not realise the wonder of the Church and her life in Christ, can be disturbed that her progress is impeded—not he who believes in Christ and His Church.

Benedict was so openly opposed to war and in favour of its being systematically abolished that a distinguished newspaper in its retrospect of his reign writes : " Benedict XV. was a convinced Pacifist." His successor, Pius XI., has declared that he identifies himself with the view of his predecessor. His solution is : " *Pax Christi in Regno Christi*." His first great Encyclical, of Christmas, 1922, " *Ubi arcano*," was a Peace Encyclical. From his watch tower he lays bare the ills of the times, the want of Faith and the disobedience to the Divine Laws, and war as the result. The Pope reminds us of the words of St. James : " Whence come war and striving amongst you ? Is it not from your covetousness ? " This inordinate greed, which clothes itself in patriotism and love of country, is to blame when, from time to time, the nations go to war. It is true that this love produces many virtues and heroic deeds, if it takes Christ's Laws as its guide (when and where is that the case to-day ?), but it becomes an evil crying for vengeance if it oversteps these boundaries and degenerates into an unbounded nationalism. Both the present Pope and Benedict XV. take their stand on the ground of

" the common obligation for all mankind in private or public life, personally or socially is to be in harmony with the Law of God," and " that it is the sacred duty of nations and governments in their political life to follow inwardly in the steps of Christ their Teacher." Here we have a repeated protest against the common theory and practice that, in political life, a moral standard may be followed quite different from the Gospel of Christ. With this Gospel in the hand, this spirit in the heart, it surely ought to be very difficult for another war of destruction to break out.

As to the League of Nations, the Encyclical takes much the same line as did Pope Benedict. It contains, however, one important hint as to the necessity of a political world organisation, when the possibility of a real Peace is considered. The Pope names two conditions : the institution of a society of men for this object (*hominum recte instituta communitate*) and the freedom of the Church for the fulfilment of her moral and religious mission.

The institution of a world-embracing organisation of justice is the work of the laws of nations. At present this is in abeyance.

" There is, to-day," says the Pope, " no human power which can bind all nations by an international code of laws, suited to the times, as was the case in the middle ages in the Christian family of the nations, which was the true League of Nations ; but there still exists a Divine Institution which can protect the Sacred Rights of nations, an Institution to which all nations belong and yet which is over them all, which is furnished with the highest authority and is worthy of reverence for the fulness of its teaching power—the Church of Christ. She alone can undertake this task, thanks to her age-long, glorious history."

It is to the Church with the Papacy at its head that the friends of Peace look with hopeful eyes.

What Benedict XV. and Pius XI. have done to improve the political outlook and to help in a lasting Peace for the world is but the beginning. Pius has grasped that flag of Peace which fell from Benedict's weary hand (" I offer," said Benedict with his dying breath, "my life for the Peace of the world ") and declared : " My life work is the work of Peace." Therefore the world must look with great expectation to the Vatican Council, which may shortly be re-opened. Even fifty years ago the Armenian Bishops implored Pius IX. to lay down rules as to righteous warfare, but the breaking up of the Council made any decision impossible.

To-day the question is far more urgent. Not only the terrible outbreak of 1914, with its poison gas and barbarous methods of warfare, but also the unrest and trouble of conscience as to the whole problem of war, cry out for an authoritative declaration.

What Francis de Victoria wrote in the sixteenth century applies equally to-day. " The Pope has authority over temporal things as well as spiritual when it is necessary for the safe-guarding of things spiritual. This is allowed unanimously. Therefore the Pope can break laws which are on the threshold of sin—such as the laws about prescription " mala fide," and on the same grounds he can give judgment between Princes who dispute as to their rights and so go to war. He can examine the rights of both parties and give a decision binding on the Princes which would prevent all the evil of a spiritual nature which must be the result of a war between Christian Princes." It may be objected that Victoria was speaking only of Christian *Princes*, but *mutatis mutandis*, his opinion applies equally to Christian citizens who are involved in similar conflicts. Suarez also teaches that the Pope, in consideration of the spiritual interests involved, has the right to deliver a binding decision on the *causa belli*. He writes : " This is what Soto tells us : ' A war between Christian Princes is very seldom justifiable because there were probably other means of adjusting their differences." The Canonist, Lupin (1496), says : " I do not doubt that the Pope, by means of punishment and censure, can forbid any war until it is proved to him to be justifiable."

An English Labour newspaper announced that the Pope would, in two years' time, forbid Catholics to take part in war (the expected Vatican Council was what they meant). This was, of course, quite an unfounded announcement, and may have been a feeler put out to sound the Press ; but many Catholics have rejoiced at such a thought when they consider the horror of modern warfare. Duelling is forbidden under pain of excommunication. Of course the comparison is unfair because, undoubtedly on both sides, a duel is unjust, whilst, in war, one side may be justified. War, however, is unjust when both the just cause is wanting and also the right ways of conducting it : when good is not furthered and evil avoided, and when the limits of justice and love are exceeded. Pope and Council, under the guidance of the Holy Ghost, can decide whether a modern war can fulfil these conditions, and whether it is possible for them to free, not only Catholics, but the whole world from the agonies of self-destruction.

CHAPTER V

PATRIOTISM

PATRIOTISM

The opposition to the principles of Pacifism rests not in reason but in sentiment. With some there may be a certain love of fighting, but with most people there is a noble sentiment involved. The Peace of the world must be subordinate to the Fatherland. " I am all for peace as long as my Fatherland does not suffer ; but if war is necessary in its interests then I am not prepared to sacrifice my country, my love for it is greater than any general love for humanity."

With most people that is the real feeling where Pacifism is concerned. We must remember that the text is not " Peace at any price," but " Justice at any price " ; yet this sentiment still prevails and merits consideration and respect. It must be purified, broadened and deepened so that it can be supported by reason and religion and made to serve a higher purpose.

Patriotism, love of one's country is universal ; but, in spite, or because of, the universality, its origin and the nature of its worth are very doubtful. The very idea involves difficulties. We speak of the land of our fathers, but in fact it is often another country that we regard as such. Is the Fatherland of the children of the emigrant that of their parents, or is it the land of their birth ?

We are treading on very thin ice when trying to define what the Fatherland really means sociologically, and what ground our patriotic feelings, wishes and dealings, have to cover, or how this love is to be qualified. These are questions of great political, and also moral, importance.

Home, nation and State, are the objects of patriotism, either separately or combined, and if combined, either all three looked upon as equally necessary or pre-eminence given to one or the other.   These are fine, but important, distinctions.

Those who stand either at the end or the beginning of their political life are the most likely to look on their own little bit of earth, where they were born, and have grown up, their own home, as their Fatherland and to centre their love exclusively on it.   This narrow home is but little concerned with political boundaries, or political considerations.   It is contained in the bit of land in the province where the homestead stands. This limited outlook is that of a man who has lived only in his own little world, but it may bring with it very bitter suffering from the outside world whose politics play with men and States like the pieces on the chessboard.   After such experiences men of all classes may go hand in hand despising all political strife, be content with their narrow little home for their Fatherland, indifferent to which flag flies over it.

This love of Home is next in strength to love of family.

Our natural love is stronger the more concentrated it is—it loses with breadth.

This intimate character of the Home stands out in contrast to the unrest of the great world and its politics. It is a little island of peace in the midst of the stormy ocean.   That is why the wanderer, at the end of his life, returns home ; that is why the home life is untouched by the passions and bitterness of the other elements of patriotism which are mixed up with the interests of State and nations.   Home is Home in spite of any changes.   Man has a tenderer feeling for his Home than he can have for the State or nation.

Nevertheless, spiritually, the nation stands higher than the Home. It is the natural Fatherland of the individual. The nation, the race has developed from the family of the same blood, the same language, customs, culture, and it is only natural that men who are so similar should also be politically united. It is war and conflict which upsets all this. Men lose their Home and their nationality and are submerged in a State that is foreign to them, but which they have to make their Fatherland.

The nation, no more than the Home, therefore, can be the Fatherland.

It is not capable of satisfying the requirements of a modern, well-ordered common existence. The common educational strength of the nation sufficed for the education of the original National States. After these States had lost their original boundaries, which were replaced by others, which were more or less arbitrary and fictitious, the principle of nationality, as a leading and constructive principle had to give way to the ordered development and perfection of the political world. To-day the spirit of nationality is more disturbing and separating than quieting and uniting. For it is more concerned with blood than with spirit and, therefore, has no calming influence, no sense of discipline or order which would make it fit to rule. The principle of nationality is full of passion. If it prevailed it would deprive all those not born of the nation, not pure bred, of the rights of citizenship which would be the extreme of injustice if we consider the mixed populations of modern countries. The modern conditions of life demand a far more universal and larger spirit. A great international central commonwealth or organisation would be the ideal of this school of thinkers. It would be paternal in its care, and would assure support, education, culture, peace and an ordered existence internationally. Nationalism is too narrow and also too wide. The members or the descendants of the same race have, in the course of history, spread over all lands, and it would, of course, be folly to try and unite them in one Fatherland, e.g. Germans in Austria or Switzerland.

From this point of view there is more to be said for the sociological sense of the Fatherland.

Two Catholic Theologians tell us that we are dealing with important, but very delicate, distinctions. Arnold Rademacher says, in his very thorough treatise on Love of the Fatherland*, " The ·Fatherland is the home enlarged, and it is as such that we treat it as an object of love." There are other ideas it is true, the geographical for instance, the mother tongue, custom and culture, but the root object of this love of country is the common organisation of the State on the State idea as the norm of this organism.

The Munich Franciscan, Erhard Schlund, says much the same. " Not Home, or people, nor State, but all three together make up the Fatherland." Still the two definitions differ, especially in the conclusions which their authors draw. If the element of the State is the most important in the love of the Fatherland then all the other elements such as race, language, culture, become secondary and must in the case of conflict be sacrificed to the interests of the State. " Therefore," says Rademacher, " if national interests clash with those of the State, the national must always be sacrificed. So in countries where there are many aliens among the citizens, any projects on their part which are in any way a danger to the State, must be suppressed."

Schlund's formula is different : " That country is only our Fatherland which is inhabited by people of

---

* *Die Vaterlandsliebe nach Wesen, Recht und Würde,* 1915.

our blood and race, who speak our Mother tongue."*

We may put this definition before us as an ideal to be realised—it may be in the future. But under present political conditions Rademacher's definition is the only practical one ; still, if Fatherland and State are identical so that every one has his Fatherland where he has settled even temporarily, a very material and perfunctory kind of love results.

If, however, the combination of Home, People and State constitutes the Fatherland, many men have none and the struggle after it must be the cause of continuous unrest and a danger to order and safety.

Yet who can doubt that the love of the Fatherland loses much of the power and warmth when the existing State, where a man happens to live, is substituted for it as a living object.

In times of Peace, when people and State are more and more drawn together there is no difficulty, but when people and State have been shattered by war and when nationalities have been changed by conquest it is hard to acknowledge the Fatherland to which duty is now owing or to feel affection for it.

Such are the consequences of identifying Fatherland and State. They are great in themselves, but they are hard to bear. Let us see if there is any solution. The tragedy lies in the fact that the three elements—Home, Nation and State—are unnaturally separated. Even where these three requisites are united into one, a neighbouring State may bring in a disturbing element if it lacks any common bond of organisation and pledge of just conduct. This produces a continuous want of security and difficulty in the mutual relationships. Just as the dwellers in one Home cannot feel peace and security if their nearest neighbours are full of mistrust and suspicion, can it not be with nations as it is with

* *Katholizismus und Vaterland*, München, 1923.

families ?   Must the love of Home and nation be sacrificed because the State gets larger and is allied with other States ?

Kant's idea was a world-wide Republic ; but as this was not practicable he hoped for a universal League of States.   This we have to-day in an imperfect condition in the League of Nations.   Rademacher says the time will come in which the League of States will have broadened into the League of the World. Then the whole world will be the Fatherland.   He adds that this very wide interpretation of Fatherland would not inspire such love as does the narrower.

That is a matter of opinion.   The present writer believes that the love of Fatherland would be intensified if it were world embracing.   Love of Home would be untouched.   It rests on the undying recollections of childhood and parents, the scenery we have grown up in, and many other things.   So the right sort of love to our compatriots, to our nation, does not depend on a wider or narrower State apparatus.

The ideal League of Nations would, of course, not suppress national idiosyncrasies unnecessarily or arbitrarily, but would protect and develop them, especially language and customs, just as the universal Church does in ecclesiastical matters.   Politically Switzerland and the United States are examples of the manifold in the one.

The ideal political unity will always have a strongly federal character.   National groups will have to make sacrifices for the good of the world.   Mutual intercourse between nations would lead to mutual appreciation and love.   Leonardo da Vinci says : " All great love is the daughter of a greater knowledge."   The most important element in love of Fatherland, statecraft, is most highly developed in the World State.   Rademacher says : " Such a League would not mean an encroachment on the frontier of any State, but an enhancing and broadening of sentiment for the Fatherland. But for this to be possible the State, not the National State, must be the object of the love of Fatherland."

In the universal State the wounds would be healed which are caused by the disruption of the three elements which constitute the Fatherland—Home, People and State. A citizen of the Universal State can lose neither his Home nor his People nor his State.

This is the ideal. Who can say if it will ever be realised.

．　　．　　．　　．　　．

The vision of a great future has been opened out, but it is just as necessary to consider the contemporary political outlook clearly and truthfully as it affects the love of country.

The first law is a decided confirmation of those obligations to which man is pledged by nature and by duty : to his Home, his Nation, his State. We will not consider his external duties to his country like service, tax paying, submission to law, etc., we are interested in the inner filial relationship of man to the State. We find two extremes : internationalism and nationalism, the belittling or the exaggeration of the national idea. Many men are rooted in a particular place. The earth itself has much to do with it. If a man has nowhere to lay his head, no home, nothing but a wretched lodging with no comfort or charm which he could find in any town the world over, if he works year in and year out in a factory and is more a machine than a man, it is no wonder that Nation and Fatherland have but little meaning for him. He only looks for amelioration in his circumstances from combination with his fellows in other countries and so he is an internationalist.

Another type of internationalist is the cosmopolitan He is more aristocratic, not fettered by squalor and struggle for existence, on the contrary he is too free and can travel all over the world, having no special home anywhere. There are certain *poseurs* of culture in society who, being really very shallow, imagine that they can do without any home or nationality. This is only a want of depth. To the argument that the vault of Heaven covers all peoples and nations alike, and the sun shines on all, and, therefore, all are alike, it may be replied that nature has made men very different, some white, some black, some brown ; we say nature, but these differences are the will and work of God. This is the truest reason for loving those of our own race and nation. God has fashioned us bodily and spiritually from our particular race, however corrupt the origin of the race may have been. This variety is a mighty factor in God's ordering of the world which He works out for His own purpose.

Each nation is a special thought of God, an expression of His wisdom, and to each has He given special qualifications, each bears the special mark of God in its natural individuality. A German, for instance, can no more become an Indian than an oak become a palm.

And men are more than trees. Men should be conscious of the individuality of their natural conditions of life. We should ponder over the special thought of God for our country, make it our own and try to fulfil it ourselves. We must unite with our fellows of the same race and blood in loving fellowship. This is only natural, it is unnatural to be spiritually transplanted into foreign soil, or to be isolated from our compatriots.

The exaggeration of nationalism is also unnatural. Though nationalism only appears late in history there is something primitive and childlike about it. As the child knows nothing outside its little circle, so the nationalist is limited to his own nation.

Concentration is good and makes for strength. The workings of internationalism just consist in this : that they do not draw enough strength from their own blood and soil and, therefore, all their productions are weak and bloodless, whilst those who are rooted deep in the soil of their own country, physically and spiritually, are strong and full of character. If every nation could develop its individuality to the full, the whole would be perfection. The nationalist also is so simple and insists so blindly on the rights and demands of his own country, and is so blind to the wants of others, that he is looked upon not as a harmless fool whose follies can be laughed at, but as a vicious and dangerous opponent, especially where it is combined with politics and culture. Even the nationalism of culture is stupid, unjust and hurtful. It consists in the belief in the superiority of one's own nation, that it is superior to the whole world, chosen by God as the salt of the earth to preserve the rest of humanity. Fichte is the typical German example of this nationalism. He is almost mad on the subject : " Only the German has really a Nation, foreigners have none. Therefore love of his country is only possible for the spirit of a German—true love of the Fatherland." Without going to such extremes it is true that a nationalist does think no nation as good as his own. If we think seriously we must see that each country has its special call from God. Material and spiritual goods, moral characteristics are dispersed over the world, and in the natural order, as the Mystical Body of the Church, no member can live to himself, suffice to himself, or lord it over the other members. The nations should be like the different chords in a symphony, making up the harmonious whole.

The great men of each nation belong to the whole world, though especially to their own nation. Was not Sophocles a true Greek, Dante a true Italian, Goethe a true German? Political nationalism rests on the false principle of race, and where to-day is a pure race to be found? Even languages cannot define a nation for political purposes. Take Switzerland, which, in spite of its various languages, is a united nation.

Saitschick tells us that the State is older than the nation and the State called the nation (the national consciousness) into being.

Nationalism, in any case, is comparatively a modern product. Antiquity knew it not, even in the days of the greatest development of the civil State. Political organisations were either a fellowship of towns or of States. Nationalism neither separates nor unites. During the thousand years of their history the Greeks only inclined to nationalism for about forty years; during the war with Persia, and during the rest of their history, nationality was the cause of bitter civil wars. In the Roman Empire a Jew, like St. Paul, was equally a Roman citizen and an inhabitant of Italy. The Jewish State was a nationalist State, but its theocratic constitution gave it a consecration which raised it above profane history; yet all the same Jewish nationalism is a proof to us how displeasing national narrowness can be in the eyes of God. Even before the Coming of Christ the Prophets, especially Isaias and Daniel, had tried to widen national consciousness into universal consciousness, but they did not succeed. Then when our Lord and St. Paul developed their supernational ideas they were persecuted by the majority of their fellow countrymen.

Their political annihilation as a nation was the punishment of God on Jewish nationalism.

How little nationalism there was in the middle ages.

We see the Neapolitan nobleman's son, Thomas of
Aquin, studying equally in Naples, Rome, Cologne
or Paris. Paul Landsberg, in *Die Welt des Mittelalters
und wir*, 1923, says that we always think of ourselves as
men or women of a particular town and place, nation
and calling, never of ourselves simply as human beings
who exist in the everlasting Being. The people of the
middle ages were just the opposite. Their nationalism
never came first. They were primarily the Redeemed
Children of God, for ever in the ordering of Eternity.

The Renaissance and the Reformation destroyed both
the oneness of Faith and the power of political unity.
This came from the exaggerated idea of the State, from
the subjectiveness of the new Religion and from the
separation of the Universities from the Church.

Each nation became a law to itself, with nothing higher
over it. As Hegel puts it, the State was the present God.
Nationalism takes the place of religion. Man must have
something to revere. States and nations provide a
higher ideal of service and awaken zeal for many high
objects : Greatness, power, a great past, a great future,
endless possibilities in fact, and it shows a noble character
to wish to sacrifice oneself for an ideal. But an ideal can
become an idol. Just as on the extreme left we see in
bolshevism, socialism run wild, so on the extreme right
we see in chauvinism what nationalism may become.
The State is practically put in the place of God, or the
old heathen cult of a national God is revived under a
rationalistic form in the New-German Church of the
new-heathen German believers !

Side by side with this acknowledged substitute is
another less recognised idolatry. Many who would be
shocked if they were told they made an idol of their
Fatherland in practice do put their country before God
and Christ. People who have no love of God are con-
sumed with love for their country. No offence against

God or the Church touches them, but they are in despair at any national misfortune.

It may be objected that moral theology allows that it is easier to experience feelings of love for some earthly good than for God ; very well, but let us test not the *affective* love of the nationalist, but his *effective* love—his wishes and deeds. " Whoso has My Commandments and keeps them, he it is who loves Me," says Christ. Does popular nationalism, then, keep the Commandments of Christ ? Is it, in times of excitement, ever unmixed with hatred and revenge and other evil passions ? There are the feelings of the man in the street. The politicians work their minds up into a considered system of blind hatred and unscrupulous lies, and even organised murder.

The gulf between the demands of Christ and the demands of political life have induced those who will not give up either one or the other to invent a double morality.

" Morality," says Treitschke, " Morality must become more political, if politics are to become more moral. Moralists must realise that the standard of State morality cannot be the same as the standard of the individual, but must depend on the aims and life of the Nation."*

This is false, for it is equally the duty of each individual or State to further God's Honour in the lives revealed by Christ. This theory of the differences between political and private morality is not a Christian product. We owe it to the Renaissance and to Machiavelli.

There is another school of Protestantism which is less honest, and which says that Christ Himself made exceptions in the Sermon on the Mount. Martin Rade†

---

* *Treitschke : Politik*, Leipsig, 1897.
† *Martin Rade im Handbuch der Weltfriedensströmungen der Gegenwart herausgegeben von Lenz und Fabian*, Berlin, 1922.

writes that under the stress of everyday necessities, Luther made a " Genial " (!) and decisive distinction between the mentality of the Christian as an individual which must be the mentality of Jesus and his mentality as a public character, which depends on the duties belonging to his worldly station. Other Protestants write in the same strain, and some more strongly.

Apart from the consequences in natural life of such a morality, it must be most demoralising to the individual, for State Officials, politicians and soldiers are ordinary human beings. If there were a special race of politicians they might have a standard of public morality whilst the ordinary man had a standard of private morality, but because the politician, the man and the Christian are all one, a double morality is subjectively impossible.

This theory of a double morality is impossible for Catholics. Martin Rade is quite mistaken when he says that, according to Catholic teaching, the precepts of the Sermon on the Mount are only " counsels," which the ordinary Christian is not bound to obey ; that the Catholic Church has two divisions, the very pious Christian—the Perfect, the Saints, Monks and Nuns on the one side, and on the other ordinary Church people. No, and in August, 1923, the Conference of Bishops, at Fulda, spoke most strongly on the obligation of the Sermon on the Mount as regards the love of our enemy. Benedict XV. said the same, as did Pius XI. in his first Encyclical.

There is no place in Catholic theory for a patriotism that insists on one morality for the Fatherland and another for private life, but many Catholics being men and patriots succumb to this temptation and divide their Christianity into Sundays and weekdays, forgetting that their Religion must go with them everywhere and always, not excepting their political life.

But would not many people laugh at the idea of subordinating all their public life to the Spirit of the Gospel ? Would they not say it would be impossible ? In Church one may cross oneself and bend the knee, but in ordinary life one clenches one's fist and elbows one's neighbour. A Catholic writer (Hauser) tells us that nationalism denies the possibility of the union of nations and a true Peace because of original sin, and it is remarkable that whilst nationalism shelters itself behind the Dogma of original sin, it forgets the Dogma of Redemption and of the renewal of the face of the earth by the coming of the Holy Ghost and the foundation of the Universal Church.

.   .   .   .   .

The word Patriotism has been misused just as much as the word Love has been misused : it is made to cover calf-love, the most brutal lust, the most crass egoism, loveless, forgetfulness of duty, or anything that stands in the way of passion—all things that are the very opposite of real Love. Patriotism can be perverted in just the same way and this is what the Church must oppose. Man must be given a higher moral standard.

Patriotism is either a moral virtue or it is not. Now a virtue must not only have a good object, but its form and subject must be good also. True Patriotism must labour for the State. If the existing form of government is not satisfactory the patriot is justified in trying to improve it by orderly and lawful means. Any unlawful opposition to lawful government is the reverse of Patriotism. It is high treason. But it is possible to sin against the virtue of Patriotism by loving our country in a wrong way.

Virtue is moderation, holding the balance between two extremes. Those fail in love of their Country who refuse to give to Caesar the things that are Caesar's. Those exceed (and often they are really wanting in patriotism) who, by their nationalism and chauvinism do not give to God the things that are God's.

The Shibboleth, " My country—right or wrong," may have a perfectly right meaning, i.e. that as children say of their parents whether they are right or wrong they are still my parents, so it can be said of one's country, but generally it is interpreted wrongly. The question of right and wrong is sunk in opportunism. It is not only a want of conscience, but also of insight, for an immoral policy always fails in the long run. Gladstone spoke both for ideal and for practical politics when he said : " What is morally false can never be politically true." It is true of the State as of the individual. What does it profit a man to gain the whole world and lose his own soul ?

This truth, which is owed to the virtue of patriotism, must influence words and thoughts. A patriotic speech, full of hatred and illwill, is filth in the Eyes of God. Also let us remember that we are patriotic or unpatriotic in our private life. Our country is one with us, if we are good we help it, if we are bad we injure it.

Love of country may be a natural or a supernatural virtue. Objectively they are the same because in each case the object is the Fatherland, but subjectively the supernatural love is much higher in cause and motive. God is the immediate cause of all supernatural virtue and endows it with His sanctifying Grace, so that it is to be used only in union with Him. Even the natural virtue of Patriotism has the moral ordering of the world, and, therefore, God its cause, for its object. St. Augustine says* if this is not acknowledged and pro-

---

* *De Civitate, Dei.*, XIX., 24.

N

claimed " there is no State, no Nation, only a crowd
unworthy of the name of Nation." How superior is
supernatural Patriotism, for it God is the Beginning
and End of the Fatherland ; it sees only with the Eyes
of God, loves only with His Thoughts and Wishes,
because He wills and as He wills. In one sense all
nations are chosen people of God because each is to
embody a special Thought of God, and has a special
task to fulfil in God's plan. Therefore each nation is
to look on itself as a member of God's great family of
the nations, and is to treat the other members with
consideration. The laws of God are above the laws of
the State, there can be no law of the State against God.
He only is a true patriot who is zealous for his nation to
resemble God, who loves what God loves, and hates
what God hates, who serves his country according to
the Will of God, not contrary to that Will.

It was thus that the Prophets loved and hated ; in
them, for the first time in history, the flame of Patriotism
burnt pure. How they loved their people. They
called them by the tenderest names—" beloved child,"
" dear son "—they offered themselves in sacrifice for
their people : " Spare them, O Lord, and strike me
instead out of Thy Book," says Moses. The Lord said
to Jeremias : " Entreat Me not for this people, do not
bring Me songs of Praise and Prayer for I will not hear
thee." And yet the Prophets thundered and stormed
at the people when they sinned and went after idols,
and forsook the true God. We learn from the Prophets
that true patriotism does not consist in denying the
sins and shortcomings of our countrymen. What
was Christ's attitude to His country ? He was a Jew
and wished to live and die as such. He loved His
nation and observed its laws and customs carefully,
but we cannot think of Him as a patriot in the sense of
a man inspired with a narrow national spirit. He sided

neither with the Roman Empire nor with the Jewish Kings. He paid taxes to the Roman State ; He called His immediate Ruler, Herod, " that Fox "; He answered the Roman Governor as shortly as possible when he asked Him if He was a King, and to all other questions He gave no answer. His Nation demanded His Condemnation because He was opposed to the national Jewish Spirit, He was not an ordinary patriot, ordinary patriotism is something quite different from the virtue of love of the Fatherland.

That our Lord possessed in the highest degree.

Jesus sought the souls of His people. These souls were led astray by national pride and envy.

Against this continued the teaching of the Prophets, which was to substitute the universal spirit for the national ; not only the Jews but all nations were to belong to Messiah's Kingdom. He treated all alike who came to Him. To Him there was neither Jew nor Greek, Bond or Free. He saw in each individual the immortal soul which was to be redeemed. Their " neighbour " was as much the heathen as their compatriot Jew. In the parable of the Good Samaritan He told us for all time the meaning of " neighbour."

For these and other reasons the Jews very soon found that our Lord was not what they considered sound in His views on nationalism. He thought just as much, if not more, of Gentiles as of His Own people—" do we not say well that Thou art a Samaritan and hast a devil ? " This was a term of reproach which branded our Lord in the memory of His people as One Who had degenerated from the teaching of the prophets and had given Himself to false teaching. It was the typical nationalist accusation of a want of national dignity. Christ had no sympathy with a patriotism that meant hatred of foreigners, and it cannot be objected that, at the time, the national feeling was not under circumstances of

high trial. The Jews' national pride was provoked
every day by the Roman Rule, but He spoke not a word
about it though He grieved for His country's
degradation.

He knew it was deserved and His Heart was open to
the soldier as it was to the Jew.   We read of two Roman
officers who, coming in contact with Him, were converted.   Of course it was His Godhead that changed
their hearts, but the medium was His Humanity, and
this is what the nationalist lacks, this Humanity, for his
love of his country repels instead of attracting.

Christian patriotism, therefore, must have Christ as
its pattern.   It is untrue to say, as the Quakers do, that
as Christ was not a soldier, no Christian must be a
soldier, for Christ would not tell His Followers to do
anything he did not do Himself.   Christ was not a
merchant nor was he married, but what is true is, that
the Christian must have the Mind of Christ and
Christian patriotism must be something that Christ
can bless.

What is most important is that it should take its
proper place—" Seek *first* the Kingdom of God and
His Justice and then the other things shall be added."
Our Home is in Heaven.

St. Augustine says, in the *De civitate Dei*, that if States
are unjust in their dealings they are no better than
bands of robbers, and if these robbers are successful
they grow into States.   A pirate, who was taken prisoner,
said, satirically, to Alexander the Great : " I, with my
little ship, am called a pirate ; you, with your fleet,
are Imperator."

The Christian's love for his country should take the
second place, subordinate to his love for the Kingdom of
God.   Only then is patriotism the supernatural virtue
which the Christian is bound to possess.

CHAPTER VI

LOVE OF MANKIND

CHAPTER VI

LOVE OF MANKIND

THIS is a term which has been very much misused. In the French Revolution, for instance, universal love of humanity was proclaimed as a new ideal, and was very convenient, as it was not necessary to trouble to love your immediate neighbour—he, especially if he happened to be an "aristocrat," could go to the scaffold in order that the far away and indefinite neighbour of low birth should be served and loved.

A more dangerous worship of Humanity, because it became a Religion, was the Positivism of Comte, Feuerbach and Zola. In place of God, it exalted Humanity as the "great being." Apart from such extremes the principle of this teaching is false, for if the general love of mankind is opposed to the love of the individual, nation or person, it is a contradiction in terms. There is really no such thing as this abstract Humanity. Just as there are individual men so there are individual nations. Love of humanity has, for its object, certain groups of the human race, or else it has no object at all. But it may be asked, though men and nations are to be loved in the concrete, cannot this love be better developed when all divisions and barriers are done away with?

It might just as well be said that if one wanted to make one's house very comfortable one should knock down all the partition walls and have one big hall like a railway station, so that all the inmates might be nearer to each other. Love does not grow by being

vulgarised, nor is it repelled by individual characteristics. The humanitarianism which comes from internationalism suffers from a misunderstanding of the
whole structure of society. All men are not equal—
some are over, some under others, and the love that
comes from God must recognise this.

There is no dull uniformity.

If everything is loved in relation to God and His
Laws then it follows as a natural sequence that those
nearest to God are most loved, as are those specially
given by God and bearing His Mark as parents and
children, husband and wife.

It is undeniable that this family love and also love of
our country and our own people must be stronger than
the love of all unknown and far away people and countries.

On the other hand, beside this specialised love, it is
possible—and it is a duty—to feel a strong and real love
for all mankind. This is the Christian law which
looks on everyone as our neighbour, even as our brother
in Christ.

The Christian love of mankind differs in many ways
from the purely humanitarian love. Firstly, in theory
at least, men are loved not for their own sakes but for
God's, in the light of the Fatherhood of God and the
Brotherhood of Christ. Secondly, this love is more for the
soul than the body. Thirdly, it recognises distinctions,
for example, our own country should be loved more than
any other. Fourthly, this love recognises the individuality of nations and does not want to level them all to a
grey uniformity, but to weld them all into an organism
with strong members and marked differences and varied
gifts. An *over*national, not an *inter*national.

We have considered the nations as members of a
great orchestra, each instrument of which is necessary
if the full harmony is to be produced.

This is a supernatural harmony, the harmony of the Mystical Body of Christ. Even if nations do not belong entirely to the Mystical Body, the fact remains that they are called to it. As Solovjeff tells us, the Body of Christ as a perfect organism cannot consist of only simple cells. It must contain also complicated and larger organs which are represented by the various nations. The character of a nation does not differ from that of one individual in any thing fundamental. It makes no difference that the nations themselves do not realise this. The individual Christian must do so. He must love the nations as Christ loved them. The Mystical Body must come first, its members must rank above his compatriots in his love if they are not members of Christ, though he must give them true love and do all he can for their Salvation. As the Body of Christ has members in all lands, the Christian's duty is to try and gather all men into that Body.

A supernatural love of mankind is possible, is even a duty for him. His love for his own country is not lessened. It is raised and illuminated. His native country is an abiding object of love for him in the Mystical Body of Christ. He knows that nationality has to give up some of its individuality by its incorporation into the unity of the Body of Christ. And, as Solovjeff says, Christianity no more de-nationalises than it de-individualises. That whole nations as well as individuals asked for spiritual new birth does not involve any destruction of national qualities and powers, only their external alteration. They are given a new meaning and a new direction. Just as Peter and John kept their individuality after their conversion—in fact it was strengthened and developed—so must it be when whole nations embrace Christianity. Weak nations, through their incorporation in the Mystical Body, become strong ; strong nations are strengthened and strengthen the weak. The fellowship with Christ penetrates everywhere and is completely satisfying. In Him we love our neighbours as ourselves—and in the same way we love every nation as our own. This in no way contradicts what has been said above, i.e., that to our own country we owe a deeper love than to any other. Love of our Fatherland has the first claim on us just as love of self comes before our love of others (Caritas ordinata incipit semetipeo). It comes first when we measure our love and unless we do measure our self-love we have no gauge by which to measure our love of others. Unless I love myself I cannot love my neighbour, for the model is wanting which is myself. All national hatred is bound up with this love of mankind. Goethe said to Eckermann that national hatred was indeed a strange thing. It is always most violent in what we may call the lowest step, but on one step it vanishes altogether and that is when we stand, as it were, above nationalism and feel the joys and sorrows of another country as our own. That love of country which some people have tried to evolve from that old nationalism will fail in these days. Our love does not make for disunion and separation, but for all possible fellowship and intercourse. The whole trend of our civilization, indeed of Christianity itself, leads to Union, combination, submission to all those social virtues which involve self-sacrifice, and the yielding even of rights which might be claimed under more primitive national conditions.

If we consider love of an *individual* foreigner, the results are the same. When we really love anyone we love what he loves. We will love his thoughts, his wishes, his belongings, even his Fatherland.

A nation requires a great misfortune to teach it that there is nothing derogatory in such love of mankind. As long as a nation can shelter its children under its wings no sympathy or love is asked for from outside, but when disaster and conquest come there rises a bitter cry for help and love from the world.

.   .   .   .

The emphasising and realisation of this Truth is the Church's special work. The Catholic must not look upon his fellow Christian as a stranger because he lives over the frontier. The Church has nothing to do with political frontiers. In Heaven all the glorified members of Christ will be closely united. Then there will be only one Fatherland, and it is a bad preparation if here Christ's members keep out of one another's way and have nothing to do with each other.

It must be the Church's work as the supernatural spiritual Home, and as the Mystical Body of Christ to overcome the nationalistic patriotism. This political nationalism is just as much an enemy to the Church as modernism, and modernism is responsible for this exaggeration of the national idea. Pius XI., in the Encyclical, " *Ubi Arcano*," says, " We have no hesitation in condemning it just as much as dogmatic modernism."

Bishop Korum, of Trier, called Chauvinism, which differs but little from extreme nationalism, " the worst heresy, an apostasy from Christianity." The Jesuit Father, Moritz Meschler, calls it " the modern demoniac possession ; the devil which destroys all the noble aspirations of man and Christian. If it is not resisted it ends in schism, but even if it does not go so far it leads to many evils."

True love of mankind and supernatural zeal for souls must never, in the future, be sacrificed to false patriotism.

The Clergy must teach their flocks that God is the Father, Christ the Brother, of all men ; and that, therefore, all mankind is one great family in God whose first and greatest commandment is love.

If this is realised by the Shepherds it will soon spread to the Flocks, and the result will be the calming of national passion.

The Christian may have to bear misrepresentation as being less patriotic than his neighbour and he must refute such accusations as the apologists of the early Church did ; but it is more important to show to the world the impossibility of reconciling the nationalistic spirit with the Spirit of Christ and His Church.

The goal is clear : to work out the ideal so that the Fatherland may reach its special God-given objective. Each individual filled with the spirit of true religion, each nation working harmoniously in the great League of Nations.

The goal is far away, but none the less clear. It can only be reached step by step. Let each patriot begin by himself becoming more holy. The fatherland is no abstraction, it is composed of the individuals who belong to it. The responsibility rests on each individual.

There is only one real love, the love taught by Christ, and the love of our country is contained in it. It must be a patient, long-suffering love, not jealous nor boasting. It must not seek its own. "Enduring all things, hoping all things, believing all things " (1 Cor., XIII.). He who loves thus, serves his country and humanity.

CHAPTER VII

PROSPECT AND RETROSPECT

CHAPTER VII

PROSPECT AND RETROSPECT

WE said, at the beginning of the last chapter, that the
opposition to an endeavour to establish a lasting universal Peace was founded more in sentiment than in reason :
but we must never forget the enormous difficulties that
stand in the way—indeed, as we look back on history,
they seem almost overpowering.

On the other hand let us remember three things :
First, let us be sure to keep the real aim of the Peace
movement before our eyes. Secondly, the duty of
fighting evil for the sake of good must not depend on
whether the object will be completely attained or not.
Thirdly, systematic work for Peace must, without
any possible doubt, have great and important results.

The Pacifist outlook has been described in this book
and the reproach that it is Utopian has been seen to be
untrue. Still, this reproach to some extent survives :
partly because the older Pacifist literature spoke constantly of " everlasting Peace." But even Kant, who
is largely responsible for the " everlasting Peace "
theory, only propounded it as the Ideal, without expect-
ing its realisation. The phrase is not found in the
modern Pacifist literature. It concerns itself to-day
with creating an atmosphere between different countries
which will unite them by the bonds of common justice.

But even if this limited Pacifist ideal appears unattain-
able is that any excuse for ceasing to work for Peace ?

We hear over and over again that it is useless to fight

against war, for there has always been, and always will be, war : a logic and morality on a level with that which decries war against sin or any evil because it has always existed. It would seem unnecessary to answer such arguments if they were not held by men who are in other respects so wise. It is our duty to oppose war just as much as any other evil, even if we cannot prevent it altogether. Otherwise men will not only be as bad, as they have always been, but each year will be worse.

Just as slavery was only put down after hundreds of years of labour by Christian men, so war will never be done away with, or even limited, but by an army of Peace workers who never cease their labours. We ask the question : is it our duty to do all we can against this terrible evil, War ? If the answer is yes, then in the Name of Civilisation and Religion we are bound to do our utmost, even though we may never stop war altogether. It is not everybody's duty to take an active part in the struggle, but no one has the right to oppose the work.

It would be depressing work if the Pacifist struggled on with little hope of success. On the contrary he must go forth, brave and full of hope, believing in the possibility of mankind.

Truly this Faith must have some supports, and they are there. Human nature may indeed be always the same, but just in this realm of society, progress has been made. In every sphere the rule of oppression has been driven back. See it in the emancipation of slaves, in the protection of workers, in women's rights. In all departments of life the appeal is no longer to force. We, under the shadow of the Great War, lose sight of this, but it is true. For instance, religious wars are unthinkable to-day. The Crusades lasted for 200 years and no European statesman could have imagined that the day would come when the question of the

possession of Holy Places would be settled with the
Turk by a stroke of the pen, and assured to Christendom for all time. The decline of religious Idealism is
to be lamented, but we must rejoice that its realisation
is no longer looked for by wars.

That is a spiritual step towards Him who said :
" Put thy sword back in its sheath."

The welding together of all mankind must be the
aim of all political work.

Suarez told us long ago that humanity, though
divided into nations and kingdoms, is still one, with a
certain political and moral unity. Francis de Victoria
tells us the same.

The Geneva League of Nations is a great step forward.
The work of construction within the League should be
" The United States of Europe." In the introduction
to *Paneuropa* Richard N. Coudenhove-Kalergi says :
" The cause of the decline of Europe, is not biological,
but political. Europe is not dying from the weakness
of old age, but because its inhabitants are destroying
one another with modern machinery. Europe is still
the reservoir of the highest in quality and the most
fruitful of the human race. It is not the people of
Europe but their political system which is senile. A
radical change in that is what will bring healing to this
smitten world." The European question resolves
itself into this : Can Europe, in its present politically
broken-up condition, maintain its Peace and its independence against the ever-increasing power of the
Asiatic nations, or will Europe be compelled, in self-
defence, to organise into a League of Nations ? This
question carries its own answer and therefore it is put
on one side, but time presses and Europe, which has
almost lost all self-confidence, looks for help from
outside—from Russia, or from America : both are
fraught with danger. Europe's salvation comes neither

O

from East nor West.   Russia would conquer it, America would buy it.   Between the Scylla of a Russian military dictator, and the Charybdis of an American Finance Dictator, a narrow path leads to a better future.   This path is called " *Paneuropa* " and means " Self-help through the union of Europe in one political and social bond " (Coudenhove-Kalergi, 1923).

But more important than all else for Europe is spiritual cleansing.   Worse than the anarchy among countries is the moral anarchy in the souls of men when it is a question of political conflict.   As we have seen in a former chapter, people, who in all other relationships, are highly conscientious have quite another political morality.   The reason is to be found in their surroundings and their education.   People abuse their political enemies unscrupulously and education, which in other respects is Christian, fails in this. The old proverb, *si vis pacem para bellum*, is still taken as Gospel.   In the old Roman world it had a good meaning, now it no longer applies.   In the old days war really led to Peace.   When tribe fought with tribe and the feud was ended by conquest, the conquered tribe was absorbed by its conqueror and so little wars were more and more prevented and the great Roman Empire gathered nearly the whole world in the mighty Pax Romana—a real world Peace.   The great difference to-day is that there is no overpowering giant that can absorb the lesser powers.   To-day all the nations stand armed to the teeth and therefore this universal readiness for war is pointless.   The truth is, if you want Peace honestly, then prepare for Peace.   Let children be brought up with ideals of Peace ; teach them the barbarous folly of war.

The educational side has not been neglected in Pacifist circles.   The German *Liga für Volkerbund* has an educational section.

The influence of the Press might be enormous. Probably ninety-five per cent. of modern people take their views from the Press. Attempts to raise Press morality are not wanting. An attempt was made in 1907 to create an international union of the principal leaders of the Press in the interests of Peace, and there have been quite a number of other attempts in the same direction.

.   .   .   .   .

In considering the problem of World Peace, from the moral and educational side, we naturally think of that greatest of all moral Powers, the Roman Catholic Church. She is the Church of the whole world and when she was in her cradle the gift of Peace was given her. The Universal Church and Universal Peace cannot be separated. Truly her first care is inward, not external, Peace, but the two cannot be divided as they act and react on each other. The Church cannot leave the world to hatred and fighting. She must fulfil her mission of Peace. Her members belong to the world as well as to her.

There are difficulties to overcome in working for Peace with non-Catholics, but let us remember our Lord's Words : " He that is not against you is for you " (St. Luke IX., 49), and non-Catholic Pacifists are with us in the work of Peace-making.

Even if no earthly powers cared for Peace the Church must always labour for it. It is her mission to heal the spiritual and bodily wounds of humanity through corporal and spiritual works of mercy.

The wounds inflicted by war are denied by no one: so it is the Church's work to heal, or better still, prevent them. To this inner duty is added an outer which is apologetic and pastoral. The Church is reproached because she has done to little to put an end to war. The masses, influenced by Socialism, instinctively turn away from an influence that they consider paints this world as a " vale of woe," and provides happiness only in another world.

They demand from a Church, if they are to listen to it, a furthering of their social interests, an honest endeavour to improve their conditions of life and a determined struggle against social evils, one of which they recognise in war. Untold harm is done by the quite false, but widely-held, idea that the Church is on the side of the great ones of the world. The result is that modern Pacifism has usurped the place of the old *Pax Christiana*, and Peace-making and the ideal of the fellowship of nations has been left to Jews and Free Masons and Internationalists. The duty of the Church is plain. All the world knows that if there were another war, not armies would be wiped out, but entire nations. Not soldiers so much as scientists, chemists and technical workers would conduct it and be its victims, and the chivalry of old warfare would be forgotten. All personal bravery would be useless. A contemporary writer says : " The next war will be conducted in silence— broken only by screams and groans of the burnt and the blinded. Past wars were conflicts between opposite artillery and engineers. The next will be unspeakably horrible, conducted by elderly gentlemen in eyeglasses who will sit in laboratories and pour out death over hills and valleys, armies and fleets and large helpless cities. Poison gas, which not only destroys the body, but unhinges the mind by fear of the unknown *Miasma* of floating deadly poison falling from the clouds like rain and spreading silently everywhere—that is the chemical war of the future. The human mind is incapable of realising the horror. Poison ships flying high in the sky will pour death and destruction on sleeping cities, fortresses will crumble like paper toys ; armies will be simply masses of tortured wrecks of humanity unable to move hand or foot." (Dr. Vito Kunz in an article, *Is another war preventable* ?)

It is a great scandal that attempts to rule out the use of poison gas in warfare should be silenced. The following points must be pressed :

1. The number of victims of poison gas is so great that it is impossible that there is any truth in the fiction that it was only used very sporadically by a few Generals.

2. Even during the war observation proved convincingly its terrible results.

3. There has been an enormous development of poison gas since the war. It is estimated that twelve bombs of a certain American gas would kill every inhabitant in a town of the size of Chicago or Berlin. This gas is heavy and penetrates into canals and springs and reservoirs so that all water would be poisoned.

Gas masks were a protection against the earlier kinds of poison gas, but later discoveries make them useless.

Dr. Kunz tells us that another war would be the death of Europe.

Is the Church to stand by in silence ? Must she not declare as loudly as she can that this wholesale murder of non-combatants is an unspeakable crime, that the making no distinction between soldiers and civilians is a violation of the laws of war of all the ages.

There we are faced with the baffling question. Can any power on earth, the Church or any other, do anything against such lust of destruction ? This question is not the first consideration—that is not *can*, but *must*. The duty is plain whatever the result.

The Church possesses immense moral means of power. She can use that power for this object as she used it against duelling. Again and again let us repeat the third and fourth conditions of a just war : that good may be furthered and evil avoided and the war be carried out within the limits of Justice and Charity.

Even in these days the Interdict and Excommunication of Rome would be powerful, and other possibilities are here. No part of the world is outside the Church. She is everywhere. The centralisation of the hierarchy with Rome becomes ever firmer and more living. At a command from Rome, French and German Bishops would confer together, the whole world would keep a day dedicated to prayers and sermons for Peace, and at every Service these Prayers would ascend to Heaven.

It is, of course, quite right that the world's, or the Church's, Peace-making should develop itself and not be commanded from outside, but all the same, discipline and organisation are not to be despised. The great objective to aim at is, the creation of an atmosphere—a Peace stream. Poor, blinded humanity must recover its sight and see that war is madness—a curse and a huge crime.

When this is realised, then is the time for Peace organisation and Peace literature.

We have seen how strongly Pope Benedict XV. felt on the subject. He desired the inauguration of a positively Christian and Catholic League of Nations. This took shape in Brussels in 1918 under the name of *La Ligue Apostolique pour le retour des nations et des peuples et de l'ordre social tout entier à Dieu et à Jésus Christ—par la sainte Eglise*. Another attempt is that of a Dutch Catholic Layman, Dr. Steger, the founder of the *Féderation Catholique Universelle*. All have received the blessing of the Holy See.

Many other smaller organisations of Catholic students exist.

The Church must teach—by sermons and catechisms. More important than all is prayer. Prayer is the way to union with God. Intercession is the way to union with our fellowmen.

Social and national enmity must be banished when class prays for class, nation for nation.

International associations for Prayer exist, and one Sunday a month is kept as the international communion Sunday. Inevitably this must breed a spirit of Unity and Charity. Other work on the same lines is being carried on in France and Germany, and has spread to South America—Chili and the Argentine are always on the brink of a quarrel : in the Andes, on the borders of the two countries, a Statue of Jesus Christ, the Prince of Peace, has been erected. The movement has the support of the Bishops of both countries and seems to have really taken root. In 1900 both countries submitted themselves to English arbitration and the imminent danger of war was averted.

If the attempt has succeeded in Argentine and Chili, why not here ? Let us call on the Bishops and Priests to help. Remember the saying : " If you have Faith as a grain of mustard seed you can say to this mountain, Remove from hence hither, and it shall remove ; and nothing shall be impossible to you " (St. Matt. XVII., 19).

" Nothing shall be impossible "—not even perfect Peace—if, in our minds, Christ is the Alpha and Omega of the Peace-ideal. *Ipse enim est pax noster.*

INDEX

ALLIANCE, Holy, 102.
AMBROSE, St., 118, 119.
AMPHYCTIONIC League, 96.
AQUINAS, St. Thomas, 57, 59, 60, 63, 64, 65, 68, 71, 76, 78, 124.
ARISTOTLE, 50.
ATHANASIUS, 117.
AUGUSTINE, St., 59, 60, 63, 64, 65, 68, 71, 75, 77, 78, 96, 118, 120, 161.
BASIL, St., 121.

BELLARMINE, 72, 75.
BENEDICT, XV., xii, 43, 84, 160, 161, 163ff., 172.
BERNARD, St., 125, 126.
BLOCK, von, 137.
BURRIT, Elihu, 104.

CAJETAN, 58, 67, 77.
CAMPANELLA, 97.
CARNEGIE, 109.
CELSUS, 116.
CHRIST—
  friend of soldiers, 87.
  cleansing the Temple, 88.
  His standards, 91–2.
  His work, 110.
CHRISTIANS—early, 113–121.
CHRYSOSTOM, St., 118, 119.
CHURCH, The Catholic (see also Mystical Body)—
  Its missionary success, 22.
  Its relation to work for peace, 111–2, 212.
  Historical attitude to war, 84–133, 158–175.
  Possible definition on war, 171.
CLAUSEWITZ, 39.
CLEMENT of Rome, 29, 33, 43.
CONSCIENCE (see also " objectors ")—freedom of, 79.

COUDENHOVE-KALERGI, 209.
CONSTANTINE, 119.
COUNCIL—of Rheims, 121
  of Toledo, 121
COURT, international, 98, 108, 109, 140, 141.
CRUCE, Emeric, 98.
CRUSADES, 123–133.
— Children's, 128.
CYPRIAN, St., 118.

DANTE, 96.
DOGGERBANK Incident, 141.

ECCLESIA, in St. Paul, 18.
EGBERT, St., 121
ENCYCLICALS :
  Ubi Arcano, 41, 172.
  Praeclara, 160.
  Pacem Dei, 161.
ENCYCLOPEDISTS, French, 99.

FENELON, 98.
FICHTE, 102, 187.
FOX, 145.
FRANZ-JOSEF, Emperor, 70.
FRIED, 98, 136, 137, 141, 144.
FULBERT of Chartres, 123.

GENEVA, 106.
  Peace Protocol, 156.
GROTIUS, 97–8.
GUERRERO, 125.
GUARDINI, Romano, 17.

HAGUE CONFERENCES, 108, 109, 138.
HARNACK, 117.
HEGEL, 189.
HENRY IV, and idea of Christian Republic, 97.
HESSEN-RHEINFELS, 98.

HILLER, Kurt, 153.
HIRSCHER, 69, 74, 116.
HOBBES, on war and nature, 49.
HUGO, Victor, 105, 139.
HUME, 99.

INTER-PARLIAMENTARY union, 107
ISIDORE, St., 120.
ISRAEL (see "Jews").

JEWS : notion of state, 18, 188, 196.
spirit of their wars, 61, 96.
the Prophets, 194.

KANT, 58, 199, 100, 101, 144, 184.
KAPP-PUTCHES, 156-7.
KEATING, Rev. J., S.J., 41.

LACTANTIUS, 115, 116, 118.
LAMMASCH, 70.
LANDSBERG, ix, 189.
LEAGUE OF NATIONS, 142, 162, 173, 184, 209.
LEIBNITZ, 99.
LEO XIII., 160.
LIGUORI, St. Alphonsus, 65.

MARTIN, St., 118.
MAURUS, Rhabanus, 121.
MAXIMILIAN I., 97.
MAXIMILIAN, St., 117.
MOLINA, 63.
MOLTKE, 52.
MYSTICAL BODY OF CHRIST, xi, 17-26.
non-Catholics and –, 23.
and humanity, 200ff.

NAPOLEON, 102.
NATIONALISM, 182ff., 203.
NEW TESTAMENT, 84-92.
NICHOLAS I., 123.
NIETZSCHE, 52.
NOBEL, 109.
OLD TESTAMENT, 59, 81.
OBJECTORS, conscientious, 78, 152.
ORIGEN, 81, 115, 116, 118.

PACIFISM—
anarchical, 78, 88.
systematic, 109.
Classic, 135ff.
Revolutionary, 137.
Religious, 143ff.
Young, 150ff.
Catholic, 168ff.
PEACE-Theories (see also Pacifism), 95-175.
In past, 95-134.
Outside church in past, 95-109.
Inside church in past, 109-134.
Societies, 103, 105, 106, 108, 149, 150, 164, 210, 214.
Congresses, 104, 105, 106, 165ff.
At present outside church, 134-158.
Inside church, 158-175.
PASSIVE resistance, 157ff.
PASSY, 105, 107.
PATRIOTISM, 179ff.
PAX Romana, 210.
Pfingst Feuer, 168.
PHILIP of Macedon, 96.
PHOCAS, 121.
PIUS X. and the War, 30, 160.
PIUS XI., 41, 172, 173, 174.
POISON gas, 213ff.
POSITIVISM, 199.

QUAKERS, 103, 145ff.

RADEMACHER, 182, 184.
REVOLUTION, French, 103.
RUVILLE, von, 126ff.

SACHSEN, Max zu, 74, 81.
ST. PIERRE, Charles, 99.
SANGNIER, Marc, 165ff.
SCHELER, xii, 33, 34, 35, 39, 58.
SEXUAL morality, 40.
SLAVERY, 50.
SOLOVJEFF, 40, 114.
STÖCKER, Helène, 153.

STRUGGLE, 48, 51.
SUAREZ, 57, 58, 62, 63, 72, 75.
SUTTNER, Berta von, 107.

TAGORE, on Europe, 42 ;
  and Christian Ideal, 74.
TERTULLIAN, 115, 116, 118.
TRUCE of God, 96, 123.
TOLSTOI, 88, 148.
TREITSCHKE, 190.

ULFILAS, 81.
URBAN II., 125.

VANDERPOL, 60, 64, 121.
VASQUEZ, 62, 63.
VICTORIA, Francis de, 57, 59, 67,
  68, 73, 77, 97, 124, 174.
VIRCHOW, 106.

WAR (see also " War, The Great ")
  —and the Church, 29, 41-3.
  and civilisation, 31-5.

WAR—(continued).
  and morality, 35-41.
  its horror, 32, 38, 213.
  its frequency, 48.
  when just, 52-92.
  in natural law, 52-80.
  defensive, 54-56.
  aggressive, 56-7.
  lawful authority, 57-59.
  just ground and intention,
    59-71.
  the true theory, 73-80.
  in revelation, 80-92.
  in Old Testament, 80-84.
  in New Testament, 84-92.
  and early Christians, 113-121.
  in Middle Ages, 121-133.
WAR, The Great—
  The Combatants, 55.
WILHELM I., 70, 160.
WILHELM II., 39.
WORLD, The, present condition,
  25, 209.